THE ANATOMY OF PROSE

---

12 STEPS TO SENSATIONAL SENTENCES
WORKBOOK

SACHA BLACK

CONTENTS

STUFF TO CONSIDER BEFORE USING THIS BOOK

If you've read the full companion book, *The Anatomy of Prose: 12 Steps to Sensational Sentences*, you'll know that I'm biased. I think *intentional* practice is the only way to improve your written word. No one enjoys the intentional practice, mind. Once I say that, there usually follows a slew of groans and eye rolls. But tough tits my friends. If you want to improve your words, do more study.

Malcom Gladwell is famed for arguing that it takes 10,000 hours of deliberate practice in order to become an expert at something. While I'm not suggesting you need to practice creating sentences for 10,000 hours before you create a decent one, I am saying that you need to put the lessons into practice. This is a workbook. There are exercises. Do them. Do them again. Then put what you learn into your manuscripts.

If you haven't read the companion book, I'd recommend you do. This is a workbook. It deliberately assumes that you've either read the full book or that you already understand many of the story building and sentence level concepts in here, which gives you the time and space to complete the exercises to help you craft the best sentences you can. If you want the detail behind the book, then you'll need to read The Anatomy of Prose cover to cover. But I've tried to add enough information to each step so that you should be able to understand the concepts and exercises.

Reasons to put this book down:

- You've come for grammar and punctuation lessons.
- You're not interested in developing your craft.
- You don't like writing craft exercises.
- You don't like dark humor or swear words.

I've tried to leave enough space for you to complete exercises in this workbook. However, you may find you need additional paper or prefer to complete some of the exercises digitally. Right then, ready to dig deep and discover how to improve your prose?

Wicked.

Let's get nitty gritty.

STEP 1 LEARNING TO SING

You might wonder why I'm starting a book about writing prose with a chapter about finding your voice. But half of voice *is* your prose. Voice is a cumulative smush of a ton of elements including: *tone, diction, style, POV (point of view), and tense.*

The sum of these elements produces a unique whole that's identifiable to a single individual. But what's more important, is finding your voice, the *heart* of *you.* The squishy soul bits that make up the deeper version of you. The parts of you that leave a mark on the people you interact with, the parts of you that people remember.

"Who you are" is at the heart of voice. Find the thing that is uniquely you and lavishly sprinkle it over your page.

By way of example, I write non-fiction fueled by sarcasm, a dark heart, and an innate and utterly persistent curiosity. Curiosity is the value that drives it. But my fiction is totally different. The voices are unrecognizable next to each other. I write fiction fueled by a sprinkling of meliorism, unwavering hope, and an obsession with death. And these differences are reflected in my voice. Those are my whys, what are yours?

One of the biggest myths surrounding 'voice' is the failure to recognize that character voice is different to author voice. Let's take J.K. Rowling. Hermione has to be one of the most famous know-it-all characters of all time. Her voice is so distinctive that I'm betting I could pull any line out of her dialogue and you'd hear her high pitched, slightly nagging, I-know-better-than-you voice. But when Rowling writes under her pseudonym Robert Galbraith in her Cormoran Strike series you hear a totally different voice—her first crime novel opens with a cold grumpy detective; a far cry from Hermione's squawking.

The point here is that a character's voice *is* their personality. It's a fundamental part of their personality and is unlikely to change throughout the story. Just because a character gets over their flaw, doesn't mean their core personality changes.

The exercises in this step are less about writing and more about personal soul searching and discovery. It's time to dig into your squishy gray matter and discover who you really are. So much of our voice is determined by our personality, by our values, and by what matters to us. What do I mean by values? I mean concepts like: *trust, knowledge, loyalty, kindness, and inspiration.*

What are your three most deeply held values?

Value 1

Value 2

Value 3

It's one thing to know what your values are, but it's another to know why they're important to you. I want you to explore why you hold those values so deeply. What is it that you find important about each value? How does the value make you feel?

Value 1

Value 2

Value 3

How can you incorporate those values into your voice? Come up with three theme sentences you could use in your books, one for each value. For example:

- You'll never win unless you learn to put your trust in others (trust value).
- Not all knowledge is worth having (knowledge / intellect value).

Value 1 theme sentence

Value 2 theme sentence

Value 3 theme sentence

Explore how you can let those values influence the word choice in your prose. For example, deciding key scenes will not have any negative words, or all romance scenes will be riddled with an undertone of mistrust. How could you reflect your values at the sentence level?

Have a look through your own work and pick out a couple of sentences that feel most like you're embodying your voice.

Sentence 1

Sentence 2

Deconstruct those sentences. Why do you think they're the most *you*?

.

.

.

.

.

.

What literary devices did you use?

.

.

.

Let's talk about the basics. There's one aspect to novel writing that has both an impact on your prose and the voice of the story. Point of view (POV).

The four POVs are:

- First person
- Second person
- Third person limited
- Third person omniscient

Do you have a preference for POV? If so, why do you like this POV? Or does your POV choice depend on the story you're writing?

.

.

.

.

Write a one-paragraph scene in your favorite POV using the following prompt: **Betrayal.**

.

.

-

-

-

-

Now write that scene in a different POV.

-

-

-

-

-

-

Now write that scene in another POV.

-

-

-

-

.

.

Now write that scene in the final POV.

.

.

.

.

.

.

Which POV did you prefer?

.

.

Why did you prefer that POV? What was it about the flow of words
and how the paragraph sounded that you liked?

.

.

.

.

Tense also plays a role in voice. Rewrite the paragraph in a different tense.

.

.

.

.

.

.

How do you feel about the new tense? Does it sound better or worse?

.

.

.

Let's look at ways you can change your voice. Write a romantic kiss scene for adults.

.

.

.

.

.

.

Now change that scene and write it for young adults.

.

.

.

.

.

.

Now change that scene again and write it for children.

.

.

.

.

-

-

Examine the three scenes you've written. What are the main differences?

-

-

-

-

-

-

What words did you remove or substitute?

-

-

-

-

How are the emotional and sensual feelings different?

-

-

-

-

Take the opening sentence from one of your favorite books and edit it. Can you make the sentence sound like your voice?

-

-

-

Take another opening sentence from a different book, can you make this opening sound like the voice of the first author rather than like yours?

-

-

-

How is your writing voice different to your current protagonist's voice?

STEP 2 LEARNING TO LEARN

Like I said in the intro, if you want to improve your prose, then you're going to have to study. Like it or not, intentional practice and intentional study is essential. Malcom Gladwell is often misquoted. The misquote is as follows: it takes 10,000 hours of practice to master a skill. But that's not exactly what he meant. See, it's not just practice you need, it's *purposeful, focused, intentional* practice that creates a master in a field. If you want to run a marathon, you don't just pull Lycra pants on and go for a jog hoping for the best; no, that will lead to a case of shin splints, runners' trots and probably projectile vomiting three miles in.

Stephen King might've said you have to read a lot and write a lot to be a writer. But he forgot to mention one key point. You need to read like a writer. Look, no one's saying you're never allowed to lose yourself in a book. That's nonsense. Of course you can. But if you want to write—and write well—then some of the time you're going to have to read with intention and focus. You'll have to stay conscious and deconstruct what the author is doing, so you can take—not their voice—but their literary tactics, tools, and devices into your own work.

That's what this step is for. It's to put you through your paces of intentionally practicing. In this step, I'll share a set of questions I usually ask myself when breaking down and studying a story. Go to your book shelf and pull off one of your favorite books or a book from your favorite author. Answer the questions in this step using it so that you start to break down the literary tactics and devices that most appeal to you. Repeated intentional practice will shape and mold your voice.

Your first task is to grab a book or two from your favorite author or authors. Go get 'em.

I'll wait.

Got one or five?

Good. Grab a glass of vino or whatever your poison is and pull up a chair. If you've already read the book open to a random page. Not the beginning and not the end. Somewhere in the middle two thirds. Read a couple of pages. As you read, "how" and "why" are your friends. When you find sentences you like, wrap your inky arms around them and gather them in. Use a pencil to underline or sticky tabs to indicate what you like or dislike. You need to keep these sentences for analysis.

Keep **how** and **why** close by—they're the basis of all good questions. Here's some questions I like to ask while reading:

- How did the author create this effect?
- How did that juxtaposition create a secondary meaning?
- Why did the author choose this point of view? Why didn't they choose another?
- Why did they choose that exact word and not another?
- How does that repetitive use of alliteration impact the flow of the sentence?

Take a paragraph, page or chapter from the book you're currently reading, or your favorite book. We're going to deconstruct it to put intentional learning into practice.

In the space below, what are your overall feelings about this author's style? Do you like their work? Are they descriptive or clean writers? Etc.

Let's go deep and look at specific aspects of their writing:

Dialogue

Did a line or a section of dialogue make you laugh? If so, why was it funny? What grammar tricks did they use to impact the timing? Or what word choices made the dialogue funny?

-
-
-
-

What do you like or dislike about the dialogue? And importantly why?

-
-
-
-

If you disliked their dialogue, rewrite a line to improve it. What techniques did you use to improve it?

-

-

-

-

If you liked their dialogue, open your WIP and see if you can rewrite a line of your dialogue using the same techniques they did.

-

-

-

-

Did you notice any patterns to the character's dialogue? Note them below.

-

-

-

-

Description

Was the author's description heavy and full of imagery or cleaner and shorter?

-
-
-
-

How do you feel about their style of prose?

-
-
-
-

Prompt questions: did the author's description evoke any feelings, memories or images in your head? Is it close to the style of prose you'd like to write?

-
-

.

.

Regardless of whether their description was heavy or clean, rewrite a paragraph of theirs. Change the description to the opposite style. If it was a clean description, make it more descriptive and vice a versa.

.

.

.

.

.

.

.

Were there any lines you thought were descriptively excellent or particularly bad? If so, rewrite one in the space below.

.

.

.

.

Now deconstruct the author's original sentence. Examine why you did or didn't like it. Look at their use of:

- Metaphors and similes
- Adjectives
- Grammar
- Repetition
- Word choice
- Anything else that stands out to you

.

.

.

.

What can you take from these reflections that you can put back into your own work?

.

.

.

.

I'm going to give you a worked example of this in practice. Instead of pasting the entire section from a book which would have me done for copyright, I'm using just a single line of prose. But you can see from the analysis how much you can learn from a single sentence.

Worked Example

> "But already the edges were rubbing off the memory's freshness. I could feel it degrading in my hands." Melissa Albert, *The Hazel Wood*.

I chose this sentence for a bazillion reasons, mostly it tickled my good bits. First of all, Albert takes an intangible concept—a memory —and makes it tangible. Hello device that we can all use *slides it in the literary knapsack*. Instead of memories, you could turn an emotion into a tangible thing by describing the texture of how it feels. Rather than stating your character feels angry, you could describe the flaming ball growing beneath his ribcage, the hot flickering edges singeing his lungs and boiling his blood.

Another way I use this method is to give an emotion a smell. I'm a total fangirl for smell in fiction because it's such an underused sense —but also smell is closely linked to memory, so it's super effective at creating imagery. This is a known cognitive phenomenon. The brain's structured so that smell neurons pass messages to each other very close to the area where your brain processes memory. The resulting effect is that you smell something and it evokes a memory. You know, like when you smell home cooked food in the street and you think of Sunday dinners at your mom's. I smell musty old books and instantly think of childhood. I'll cover this in more detail later.

You could make your character's anger tangible by describing the scent of ash and burning rubber or perhaps the taste of hot bile in your prose. The options are limitless.

The other reason I underlined this sentence is because it took a familiar concept—memory—and used it in a unique way to create characterization.

Some of the most wonderful characterization comes from the details that only that character notices. In this instance, the character (Alice), notices how memories fade. Of course we all know memories fade, but it's the fact she draws attention to the detail of it degrading that shows insight into her character.

Albert also poses two juxtaposed words against each other: freshness and degrading. These two used in close proximity create a rich imagery effect in themselves.

Last, I wanted to pick up on the specific use of the word degrading. That single word choice created a picture in my mind where I could see a translucent orb in a hand with frayed edges and pieces breaking off in the wind. I'll talk more about the power of word choice later. But I wanted to highlight it specifically here.

Holy shit balls guys, one quote created an entire page of lessons and reflections. This is why the exercise of reading with purpose is so important. If we can learn that much from a single quote, imagine how much we can learn from 10 books' worth of quotes.

Characterization

Review the characters in the last book you loved and enjoyed. In the space below, write down why you thought those characters were so good.

Prompt questions:

- What was it about the characterization that you loved?
- What stuck with you?
- Were there any particular lines of dialogue you remember?
- Was it a particular part of their personality or the way they described things?

•

•

•

•

•

•

•

Choose one or two particular lines that capture one of your favorite character's personalities. Deconstruct those lines. Prompt questions:

- What element of their personality is this line displaying?
- How is it displaying that aspect?
- What words in particular denote the personality aspect?

•

•

•

•

•

Create a new character with the same trait(s) as your favorite character from the book. Write a scene displaying the character trait and use one of the same literary techniques the author did. You're not allowed to use the same descriptive words—words like *a, the, and, that,* etc. are allowed.

-
-
-
-
-
-
-
-

Internal Thought

How does this author use internal thought? Do they make frequent use or limited use? What are they achieving with their usage of inner thought? For example, are they deepening the characterization? Are they giving information away? Or something else entirely?

-
-

What does the character's inner thought or narration tell you about their personality?

Review the other characters in the story. Identify an occasion where one of the main characters made a comment, observation or insight into a *secondary* character that made you stop and think or see that secondary character in a different light. What was it about that comment that made you view the character in a different light?

Deconstruct the observation. What technical tricks or literary devices did the author employ? What literary devices or tools did the author use to create the effect?

-

-

-

-

Technical Observations

Here, this is mostly about the nitty gritty technicalities of writing. The functional structure of sentence devices like metaphors and similes or juxtapositions.

Foreshadowing

If you haven't already, read the book from the above section in its entirety. If you didn't pick any out during your read, go back and look for three instances of foreshadowing. Note in the sections below what type of foreshadowing the author used e.g. emotional, plot, character development, an omen, something else. Write down the foreshadowing sentence.

Foreshadowing 1 type.

Foreshadowing 1 sentence noticed.

Foreshadowing 2 type.

Foreshadowing 2 sentence noticed.

Foreshadowing 3 type.

Foreshadowing 3 sentence noticed.

Juxtapositions

Find an occasion where the author used a juxtaposition. Copy the sentence out below:

-

-

-

What about the sentence is juxtaposed? Deconstruct the sentence. What do you like or dislike about it?

-

-

.

.

General Sentences

Note down three sentences from the book that you pencil-marked, sticky tabbed or noted. They can be good or bad sentences.

Sentence 1

Sentence 2

Sentence 3

For each sentence, answer the following:

- Was it a good or bad sentence?
- What about the sentence stuck out to you?
- What devices did the author use to create the effect in the sentence?
- Do you have any other thoughts about the sentences?

Sentence 1

Sentence 2

Sentence 3

Sentence Level Observations

Sentence level observations often blur with technical observations, though I'm separating them here so it's clear that you should look for additional things. Sentence level observations include things like:

- The use of parenthesis in narrative.
- The intentional overuse of commas.
- The use of em dashes to add extra insight or break complex sentences down.
- The use of footnotes or asides for either humor or worldbuilding or other reason.

Thinking about the novel in its entirety, and using the list above as a starting point, write some notes about what sentence level devices the author has used.

How do those sentence level devices affect the author's prose? Write your observations below.

How do these devices and uses of sentence levels tricks impact characterization?

Flash Fiction

I'm a firm believer that flash fiction can and will change your writing for the better. Sometimes the most powerful stories are those told in just one sentence. I'm sure you can recall a tagline that punched you in the gut and made you buy a book immediately. When you only have 99 or 299 words to play with, you have no choice but to be creative with words. Every word counts—you're forced to remove any toe-fluff and self-indulgent ramblings, and that gives you cleaner, bolder sentences. The important thing about flash fiction is that it must have a beginning, middle and end.

Even if you're resistant, just have a go. You'll be amazed how much your writing will improve when you're constrained by a word limit. Here's an example of a piece of flash fiction I wrote that won a Reedsy writing competition back in November 2018:

Love isn't supposed to start with death. But nothing good ever started with rules. I don't know what makes me move. Maybe it's the fear etched into the furtive glances he gives the gravestone. Or maybe it's the cold penetrating loneliness settling in my chest. But my feet betray me, abandoning my husband's fresh grave to carry me through the cemetery toward him.

"I'm sorry for your loss," I say.

I hate that phrase.

He stands, and a string of words tumble from his mouth, the sounds and syllables melding together like molten lava. I have no idea what he's saying, but it's beautiful. We skip through a handful of languages until we reach a broken Spanglish and establish our tears:

His wife, my husband. Both dead; both cancer.

In the end, we don't need words to understand each other's pain. It's written in the slant of our shoulders and the weariness of our expressions.

Love and death are spoken in heartbeats and silences, wordless promises and unspoken goodbyes. And sometimes, just sometimes, in the flutter of hope captured in the gaze of chocolate brown eyes.

Write a story in less than 250 words. Your prompt is: death.

-

-

-

-

-

-

-

-

-

-

-

-

-

-

Write a story in less than 99 words, your prompt is: knife.

-

-

.

.

.

.

.

.

Write a story in less than 49 words, your prompt is: giggle.

.

.

.

.

.

.

Write a story in one sentence, your prompt is: love.

.

.

.

STEP 3 WHERE WE COCK UP IN STYLE

Part of developing your craft is understanding the things we do wrong. Though I'm loathe to say that any one thing in prose is wrong. There are no rules. But there are some devices and tactics that make your writing that much slicker and tidier.

If you can identify what's wrong, then you'll know how to avoid it. So in this step, you're going to make purposeful mistakes and then correct them. In doing so, you'll see the differences between good prose and shoddy prose and understand what techniques will improve your sentences.

Anchoring

Take the opening two paragraphs from a chapter in one of your works in progresses (not chapter one or two). In the first paragraph, without the context or knowledge of the previous chapter:

Can you tell who the POV character is?

.

-

What the time of day is or how much time has passed?

-

-

Where the characters are located physically?

-

-

If you can identify each of those things, then congratulations, your chapter is anchored. For those with a fully anchored chapter opening, rewrite the first paragraph so it is no longer anchored. It's important to see what openings look like without anchoring.

-

-

-

-

-

For those who had a chapter opening that wasn't completely anchored, rewrite it so that it's fully anchored.

-

-

·

·

·

Repetition

Write a short paragraph describing an old Victorian mansion. The paragraph must describe the building fully, but I want you to purposefully repeat yourself a couple of times; describe the same aspects of the building in different ways.

·

·

·

·

·

·

Rewrite the paragraph removing the repetition.

·

·

·

·

·

·

Write a sentence or two with as many similar descriptive aspects as possible, for example using 'hum' 'vibrate' 'rumble'. Your prompt is: old man.

·

·

·

·

·

·

Now rewrite the sentences without a single element of repetition.

·

·

·

·

.

.

Review your manuscript, current WIP, or character notes. Do you have any characters performing similar roles? i.e. two mentors. Are there any duplicated personality traits or archetypes? Record your thoughts and findings below.

.

.

.

.

.

.

Write a list of your top 20 (if you have that many) character's names. Review the names do they start with a range of letters? Or have you got an unconscious bias for a particular letter of the alphabet?

.

.

.

.

.

.

.

.

.

.

.

.

Check your first 15 scenes or chapter openings. What do they open with? Dialogue, description, thought, action? Something else? Record how each one starts below.

1.

2.

3.

4.

5.

6.

7.

8.

9.

10.

11.

12.

13.

14.

15.

Do the same for the ending of those first 15 scenes or chapters. How do they close? Dialogue, description, thought, action? Something else? Record how each one ends below.

1.

2.

3.

4.

5.

6.

7.

8.

9.

10.

11.

12.

13.

14.

15.

What does this show you? Do you have a series of repeated openings and closing? Or do you have a balance of styles?

.

.

.

Crutch Words

Run your current WIP through a word frequency checker online. Other than the obvious words that are always used a lot like: *I, she, that,* what crutch words have you used? Common crutch words include: *just, but, so, that, look, hand, eye, glance, walk.* Write your personal list of crutches below:

-

-

-

-

-

-

Now review the frequency checker for descriptive words. What have you used more than three times? Write a list below so you're aware of your descriptive crutches. Note that the more unusual the word, the less frequently you can use it before it becomes obvious repetition to the reader.

-

-

-

-

-

-

Redundant Words

Write a sentence using the following prompt: disagree. Make the sentence as wordy as possible.

.

.

.

Now rewrite that sentence making it as clean and short as possible.

.

.

.

Clichés

Write a sentence using the cliché 'just in the nick of time'.

.

.

.

Now rewrite the sentence without the cliché, which one sounds better?

.

.

.

Filtering

Filtering is when you, the author, add in unnecessary narration, causing the reader to be removed one step from the character, for example, phrases like:
- I heard
- I saw
- I felt
- I thought

With Filtering:

I **heard** an owl hooting in the trees and a moment later I **saw** the canopy leaves rustle as if replying.

The reader doesn't need to read the word "heard" or "saw" because it's implied in the description of the sound.

Without Filtering:

An owl hooted in the trees, a moment later the canopy leaves rustled as if replying.

Write a short scene in first person POV. Your character is in a forest looking for something. Use as many instances of filtering as possible.

.

.

.

.

.

.

Now rewrite the scene removing every single instance of filtering.

.

.

.

.

.

.

Review both scenes, which one did you prefer? And why?

.

.

.

.

ING and As

Go to a random page in the middle of your manuscript. Count how many times you've used *ing* or *as* on that page. Note the number of uses and the specific words you've used in the spaces below.

Ing uses:

As uses:

Rewrite the page and remove as many instances of *ing* and as possible.

-
-
-
-
-
-
-
-
-
-

.

Now review the two versions, which version do you like more and why?

.

.

.

.

Conflicting Description

Conflicting description creates an impossibility for example:

The lion cub sat in the dawn light listening to her father's roar softly drifting across the desert plains.

A roar, be it from a cub or a fully-grown lion cannot be quiet. By its nature, a roar is loud. Therefore, this description is illogical. Illogical descriptions create cognitive dissonance in the reader's mind.

Write three different sentences with conflicting descriptions.

Sentence I

.

.

.

Sentence 2

.

.

.

Sentence 3

.

.

.

Now rewrite those sentences without the conflict.

Sentence 1

.

.

.

Sentence 2

.

•

•

Sentence 3

•

•

•

Taking Action Out of the Present

In *The Anatomy of Prose* textbook, I use the following example of taking action out of the present:

"Julie replayed her argument with Frank so much that night she didn't get more than two hours sleep."

The action of replaying her argument happens before 'now' in the story. It occurred last night but Julie is telling you about it now. Therefore, the action has been removed from the present.

Rewrite this sentence and put the action back into the present.

•

•

•

.

.

Now rewrite it and expand it into a flashback.

.

.

.

.

.

Adverbs

Write a sentence about a child playing a game using at least three adverbs.

.

.

.

Now remove all of the adverbs.

.

-

-

Which sentence sounds better and why?

-

-

-

Write a short scene only using dialogue. Your two characters are discussing a misplaced envelope full of cash. Use adverbs in your dialogue tags e.g. she chortled.

-

-

-

-

-

-

Rewrite the scene without the adverb tags.

-

.

.

.

.

.

Which scene do you prefer? And importantly why do you prefer that scene?

.

.

.

Passive Voice

In the passive voice, you make the recipient of the action the subject and the person or agent doing the action the object. For example:

Active Sentence:

The dog chewed the bone.

Passive Sentence:

The bone was chewed by the dog.

Now write a sentence about a cat using the passive voice.

-

-

-

Rewrite the sentence making it active.

-

-

-

Analyze both sentences, which one sounded better and why? Did one feel awkward?

-

-

-

-

STEP 4 SHOW ME THE MONEY... I MEAN STORY, BABY!

"Show, don't tell" is one of the original debates in story history. The concept originates with the Russian playwright Anton Chekov. Though different to his original words which were sent in a letter to his brother, the bastardized and subsequently popularized quote goes something like this:

> "Don't tell me the moon is shining; show me the glint of light on broken glass."

Regardless of what he said, I'm tired of debate all together. "Show, don't tell" started as a great piece of general guidance to err on the side of showing when trying to evoke imagery. "Show, don't tell" isn't about discarding one technique for the other, it's about understanding the differences between them and when you're better placed using show rather than tell or vice versa. In crude terms, the best way to know whether you should show or tell is to ask one question: **is this moment, detail, or scene significant or important to the story, plot, or character?**

Examples of Both Showing and Telling

- **Narrative Telling:** Fred was furious.
- **Narrative Showing:** Fred clenched his fist, his neck flushed first red then deepened to a rich, plummy purple.
- **Dialogue Telling:** "You're just bitter, Mary. It's not a good look on you."
- **Dialogue Showing:** "For Christ sake, Mary. Parading tea and scones out doesn't hide the contempt. I can see right through you and so can she."
- **Describing Telling:** The car was old and rusty.
- **Describing Showing:** The sun had bleached the red out of the car's roof, it was more pathetic tangerine than sports car red. The hood was in an even worse state than the roof; it was blistered with such angry brown patches I swore the whole thing would flake away in a single gust of wind.
- **Inner-thought Telling:** *John was right, I didn't like Sue because I'm jealous of her.*
- **Inner-thought Showing:** *John was right, I didn't like Sue. She was too busy slapping paint on her face and pouting her lips for the cameras to be a nice human.*
- **Setting Telling:** The beach was warm and sandy.
- **Setting Showing:** My toes sank into the sand, the occasional shell fragment dug into my heel but I didn't mind. The sun was streaming over my face with the kind of fresh warmth you only get by the ocean.

So now you know the difference between showing and telling, when should you do each one?

When to Tell:

- Action scenes
- Where there's a need for pace
- Avoiding scene or narrative repetition
- Shifting scenes
- Younger protagonists

- When it's in character
- Reader attention
- Complex worldbuilding
- Avoiding narrative repetition

When to Show:

- Emotional scenes
- Important pivotal scenes
- Areas you want to draw your readers' attention to
- To slow down the pace
- Characterization
- Worldbuilding
- Foreshadowing

Let's get into the exercises.

Pivotal or Emotional Scenes

Take a key scene you're working on, be it an emotional one, a pivotal plot point or otherwise. Key scenes typically require more description to convey their significance and therefore need more showing. Answer the following questions:

What insight, meaning, symbolism or image do you want to convey to the reader in this scene?

.

.

.

.

.

.

What new insight, change or detail do you want to tell the reader about your character or their personality specifically?

.

.

.

.

.

.

What aspects of the world do you want to enrich with description?

.

.

.

.

.

.

Think of two metaphors you could use in this scene.

-

-

-

-

-

If you need to foreshadow something in this scene, what symbolism, juxtaposition or other device could you use to create the foreshadowing, use the space below to throw down some thoughts.

-

-

-

-

-

-

Rewrite one of your own paragraphs to see if you can create three versions:

One descriptive, slow version.

-

-

-

-

-

-

One middling-length paragraph.

-

-

-

-

-

-

One short, sharp version.

-

-

-

-

-

-

Reflect on those scenes, which version do you prefer and why?

-

-

-

-

-

-

Action Scenes

Take a scene in your climax or a scene where there's a lot of action. What action do you need to convey?

-

-

-

-

Are there any emotions or feelings or foreshadowing you need to convey?

-

-

-

-

Write the scene below:

-

-

-

-

-

-

-
-
-
-
-
-

Edit the scene, trimming back as much description and wordiness as possible.

-
-
-
-
-
-
-
-
-

·

·

Edit the scene to add as much description as possible.

·

·

·

·

·

·

·

·

·

·

·

·

How has this changed the pace and tension in the scene?

-
-
-
-

Edit the scene one last time, play with the level of description and cleanliness. Make sure you have both pace and one area where you slow down time and pace in your scene.

-
-
-
-
-
-
-
-
-

.

.

Try and write the following types of sentences in both a showing and telling format:

Dialogue Showing:

Dialogue Telling:

Setting Description Showing:

Setting Description Telling:

Character Description Showing:

Character Description Telling:

Inner Thought Showing:

Inner Thought Telling:

Narrative Showing:

Narrative Telling:

STEP 5 CHINWAG CENTRAL

Despite what you might think, dialogue in fiction is not about creating a realistic conversation. So then, what is dialogue? For a long time, I was happy in the knowledge that dialogue was "spoken"—albeit in fiction—language. But I read *DIY MFA: Write with Focus, Read with Purpose, Build your Community* by Gabriela Pereira, and was taken with one particular quote:

> "Dialogue is communication between characters, not communication between the writer and reader. Do not confuse the two." Gabriela Pereira, *DIY MFA: Write with Focus, Read with Purpose, Build your Community*.

Realistic Dialogue

Dialogue is weird. See, we *think* it's meant to be realistic. But realistic dialogue would read horrendously. This is how a real conversation written in fiction would sound:

"Darling?" I say trying not to sound whiny.

"Hmm...?"

"What do you want for dinner?"

"Oh, errr, I don't know. Umm...I—" she's not even looking at me.

"Come on, babe, I always have to choose..."

"Well... I don't... I can't think of anything. What do you want?"

'For god's sake, Jules."

"Jesus, calm down... Umm, what's in the fridge? Did you get cat litter today? The cat needs biscuits too."

"I dunno, yes and yes. Can you—Hold on one second... Look can you just go and check? I'm trying to finish this email."

Real dialogue is full of interruptions, half thoughts, umm and erms and is horrendously convoluted. Dialogue in fiction needs to be so much more than dialogue in real life. For example, you could rewrite the above scene in three lines, like this:

"What do you want for dinner, Darling?"

"No idea, what are the options?"

"Can you check the fridge for me? I just need to finish an email."

Write a realistic conversation between two characters about their weekend.

.

.

.

.

.

.

·

·

·

·

·

·

Now edit this dialogue to make it appropriate for fiction.

·

·

·

·

·

·

·

·

·

Dialogue Tags

Dialogue tags are the words that come immediately after dialogue ends, such as: she said, he says. These tags are better left simple as in: says and said. However, lots of writers will complicate tags by adding descriptive words like: she laughed, he coughed, she chortled. But "said" is spectacular, it has magic powers. It's the unicorn of grammatical spanners. It's a word that readers are blind to. They skim over it, which makes it one of the only words you don't have to worry about repeating—*all hail the merciful repetition gods*. The problem with using fluffy dialogue tags is that they like attention. Specifically, the reader's attention which is drawn to the tag because it's unusual and unexpected; it's not their good ol' buddy said. Whenever the reader's attention is drawn in this way—like with exposition—it reminds them they're reading. They become aware of the technical craft of writing rather than being absorbed in the flow of the story.

Write a piece of dialogue where every line has a descriptive dialogue tag. Your prompt is: fish.

.

.

Now write the same scene removing every dialogue tag.

.

.

.

.

.

.

.

Review the scenes. What you feel about them? Is one confusing? Is one awkward?

.

.

.

.

Rewrite the scene one last time striking a balance, aim to keep the dialogue tags as simple as possible.

-
-
-
-
-
-
-

Dialogue Beats

Dialogue beats are different to tags. They describe a physical action or movement a character makes while speaking, or between bouts of speaking. Here's an example from the third book in my Young Adult fantasy series, *Trey*:

> "Hermia glugs the rest of the tumbler and takes the rapidly diminishing bottle of Mind Numb from me.
>
> 'Well,' she says, pouring herself another glass, 'are you?'
>
> I swill my glass, watching the liquid lick up the side. I raise it but pause. 'No.'" Sacha Black, *Trey*.

The action of Hermia pouring herself another drink between the words "well" and "are you" is a dialogue beat. Beats are great for keeping the pace of dialogue varied. It keeps the action going and brings depth and life to long sections of dialogue. However, there's a temptation to over use beats. Just as interrupting dialogue frequently can be distracting and irritating for readers, so too can the overuse of dialogue beats.

Write a short scene using dialogue only. Interject each line of dialogue with a dialogue beat. Your prompt is: the office.

-

-

-

-

-

-

-

Rewrite the scene still using only dialogue. Remove all dialogue beats.

-

-

-

-

-

-

-

Review both scenes, what do you like or dislike about each scene?

-

-

-

-

Rewrite the scene one more time, this time striking a balance between dialogue tags and beats.

-

-

-

-

-

-

-

Reflect on this last scene, what do you feel about all three versions? What works for you?

.

.

.

.

Names in Dialogue

There's one common mistake I see in manuscripts: characters using each other's names or nicknames in conversation. For example:

"Listen, James, I don't think you should go in there..."

"Come on, Mike, it's just a bit of fun. It's been empty for years."

"Yeah, James, that's the point."

"What are you, Mike, chicken?"

"No, James, I prefer realist."

Are you screaming yet?

Here's an exercise: go find your partner, or your child, or a random stranger on the street. If you don't know their name, ask for it. Then use it in every sentence in your conversation. What you'll find is that after a sentence or two, you'll rapidly feel awkward. That's how it reads in prose too. If you happened to pick a stranger, then accept my apologies in advanced, you may well get a bop on the schnozzle.

When you use a person's name repeatedly, it creates a patronizing and mildly aggressive tone of voice. Why? Well, if you're talking to someone you know, then you *know* their name. Why do you need to use it? Using a person's name is reserved for those who are unfamiliar with each other, when your mom is full-naming you, or if your character is being rude and trying to make a point.

Write a scene where you use character names repeatedly. Your prompt is: festering.

-
-
-
-
-
-

Now rewrite the scene and don't use any names directly in the dialogue.

-
-
-
-
-

.

.

Reflect on both scenes, what do you think about each one? Which one feels better? Where do you feel the balance is? What will you take from this exercise going forward?

.

.

.

.

The Pace of Dialogue

If you want to create specific effects with your dialogue like arguments, then you need to employ particular tactics to change how the dialogue reads. When someone is angry or shouting, they're more likely to spit short sharp sentences, so using more full stops and shorter sentence lengths will help create that effect in your prose. For example:

"How could you?" she spat. "It had nothing to do with you. This was about me and her."

"Sal, listen—"

"No. You've done enough. Don't try and fix this. You weren't there."

If someone is thoughtful, in a less formal situation or more reflective in their argument, they're more likely to have longer flowing sentences. In this instance, lengthen your sentences by using more commas to represent the flow of thought. For example:

> "It had nothing to do with you, it wasn't your fight," I knead my head trying to ease the dull thump that's clawing at my temples.
>
> "This was about me and her and our inability to be honest with each other. How are we supposed to do that now? You told my truth before I had a chance."
>
> "I'm sor—"
>
> "No. It doesn't matter what you say now. She'll never believe I was going to tell her."

Having more flowing, lengthy dialogue not only changes the tone of the speaker but the tone and pace of the argument too. When you come to write dialogue, always consider the tone you're trying to create and how playing with punctuation and sentence length can impact your prose.

Write a pacey argument in the space below. The prompt is: money.

.

.

.

.

.

.

.

-

-

-

-

-

-

Now rewrite the argument making it much slower and more thoughtful.

-

-

-

-

-

-

-

-

-

-

-

-

-

Reflect on both of these scenes, which scene did you like? What tactics did you use to create the pace and to slow it down? What techniques have you learnt that you'll use going forward?

-

-

-

-

Contractions

The use of contractions in dialogue is even more important than in prose. If you're writing historical fiction or you're trying to create a specific effect, like a stiff or pompous character, then this advice won't apply. However, if you're writing a story set in modern times or with modern language, then I urge you to use contractions in speech. We're a lazy ol' bunch of humans and despite our ability to endlessly waffle, our natural speech pattern is to reduce words, cut corners, and be efficient. The fastest way to do that is to use *don't* rather than *do not*.

Write a scene predominantly using dialogue, use the prompt: "we're late". *Only* use contractions.

·

·

·

·

·

·

·

·

·

Now rewrite the scene removing all the contractions.

·

·

·

·

·

·

·

.

Review both scenes, which one do you prefer and why? Which one feels more natural? Which one flows more?

.

.

.

.

Differentiating Characters in Dialogue

Writers often worry that their dialogue all sounds the same, but there are lots of prose tricks you can use to differentiate between your characters. Remember, **dialogue is no longer your voice as the author or narrator, dialogue is your character's own voice.** So it's important to reflect that difference in the tone and style of dialogue. Start by asking:

- Where your characters come from (do they have an accent?).
- What type of background does your character have?
- Are they formal or colloquial in their demeanor?
- Do their jobs give them a more nuanced vocabulary?

I've exaggerated the below example for effect, but you get the picture:

"I refuse to discuss the matter further. Whether or not you pulled your gluteal tendon during last night's exploits or not is not appropriate dinner conversation."

Let's change the type of character entirely and have someone who uses lots of slang:

"Nah, mate, I ain't sittin' here chatting shit about yo' ass cheeks cause ya banged a pussy an couldn't handle it."

Write a short scene below where the two characters have drastically different accents. Your prompt is: teacher.

.

.

.

.

.

.

.

.

.

Rewrite the same scene, only this time make one character use formal language and one use slang.

.

-
-
-
-
-
-
-

Misunderstandings are also useful tricks to put in your prose. You can often create misunderstandings by leaving key bits of information out. You can also utilize silence or the lack of response to allow your character to come to their own conclusion. Write a romantic misunderstanding below, make sure you use the tricks I just mentioned.

-
-
-
-
-
-

.

.

.

Inner Monologue

Inner monologue occurs when a character expresses their inner thoughts or feelings. Usually, you'll find it formatted in italics to differentiate it from spoken out loud dialogue or narration. And while we're talking formatting, you don't use quotation marks for inner dialogue, EVER.

Write a scene in your current manuscript where your protagonist is deep in thought, has a realization or an emotional revelation. Ensure you *overuse* inner monologue, using it multiple times.

.

.

.

.

.

.

.

.

Now rewrite the scene removing every instance of inner monologue.

.

.

.

.

.

.

.

.

.

Rewrite the scene one last time, this time creating a balance of inner monologue.

.

.

.

·

·

·

·

·

·

STEP 6 WORD DELICACIES

I hate tuna. My son, however, loves it: like all things in life, one person's love is another's hate. Word choice creates the same love-hate feelings in readers. Some love flowery prose, others prefer a cleanly shaved sentence.

Better verb and descriptive word choices create more intense imagery and often require fewer words too. Don't assume if you use a verb and avoid adverbs, that you're winning. I wish it were that simple. There are a lot of bland verbs that only evoke basic imagery. The more specific a word is the sharper the imagery it creates. Let's look at some examples:

Poor Words:

Even though his arms were **weak**, he **held** the baby and **sang** to her.

Strong Words:

Even though his arms were **limp**, he **cradled** the baby and **whispered** a dreamy lullaby.

Write a descriptive sentence with the blandest words you can.
Describe a wolf.

.

.

.

Now rewrite the sentence swapping out the bland words for specific
or strong verbs and words.

.

.

.

We derive meaning not just from logic, but from observation and
from association which is assisted by the heuristics we develop in
childhood. Let's play a word association game. Here's a word: rain.
Write down the first eight words that spring to mind. Go on... I'll wait.

.

.

.

Done it? Cool, here were mine:

Cold, drenched, flood, soaking, wet, miserable, shower, thunderstorm.

Write a sentence using those words.

.

.

.

I'm betting your sentence has negative connotations or is a more negatively angled sentence. But rain can be viewed positively if you choose. For example, here are some positive words connected to rain: *spring, dew, buds, fresh, cool, breeze, green, plants.*

Write a new sentence using this set of words.

.

.

.

Review both sentences, is the second one more positive than the first? What can you take from this exercise into your prose going forward?

.

.

.

Verbs create movement in sentences because of the associations our brains draw from them. Verbs describe an action which creates movement in the story and prose because the brain makes associations with both the words in the sentences and the heuristics in our heads. That's why 'meander' creates a better image than 'walk'.

For each weak verb below, create a list of strong verbs you could replace it with.

Weak Verb: walk

Strong Replacement Verbs:

1.

2.

3.

4.

5.

6.

7.

8.

9.

10.

Weak Verb: ask

Strong Replacement Verbs:

1.

2.

3.

4.

5.

6.

7.

8.

9.

10.

Weak Verb: run

Strong Replacement Verbs:

1.

2.

3.

4.

5.

6.

7.

8.

9.

10.

Weak Verb: talk

Strong Replacement Verbs

1.

2.

3.

4.

5.

6.

7.

8.

9.

10.

Specific vs Vague

The less specific a word is in your description, the vaguer the sentence is. Vague sentences don't give readers much to work with. It's harder to create imagery with vague sentences and word choices and therefore harder to connect to the story. But equally, having paragraph after paragraph of detail and specific word choice can be a chore to read. A balance of the two—like all things in literature—is important.

If you want to describe something and create an image in a reader's mind then using more specific wording will achieve that faster. Let's look at three increasingly specific examples:

Example 1:

He was average height with brown eyes and a hard stare.

Example 2:

He slipped through the crowd unnoticed, his height allowed him to slide behind taller heads and bodies. I caught his intense brown eyes and faltered. They were so dark they were almost black.

Example 3:

He was of average height—average everything, to be honest. Except his eyes. They were such a dark brown they almost looked black. But what struck me was what they held, a knowing; he'd seen death. *No.* I glanced again. It was darker than that. His eyes called to death, clutching it like a play thing. I stiffened as he passed and vowed never to cross him.

Create a vague description of one of your characters.

.

-

-

-

-

Now edit that description to make it as sharp, focused and specific as possible.

-

-

-

-

-

Review both descriptions, which one create the most imagery in your mind?

-

-

-

First and Last Lines

First and last lines are tricky to get right. One great method of learning what works is to collect examples of things you think work.

Use the space below to note down 10 of your favorite book's first lines.

1.

2.

3.

4.

5.

6.

7.

8.

9.

10.

Use the space below to analyze the lines. Are there any similarities in voice, literary devices used etc.?

-

-

-

-

-

-

Use the space below to note down the last lines from the 10 books you used in the above examples.

1.

2.

3.

4.

5.

6.

7.

8.

9.

10.

Use the space below to analyze the lines. Are there any similarities in voice, literary devices used etc.?

·

·

·

·

·

·

STEP 7 DESCRIPTIVE PROSE

I'm going to start with a quote:

> "Rich, engrossing description is a mysterious combination of imagery, detail, and word choice." Gabriela Pereira, *DiY MFA: Write with Focus, Read with Purpose, Build your Community*.

I love this quote because it's so true. The art of good description is somewhat mysterious. You can mix those things in a number of ways and sometimes you get cake and other times sunken soufflés. There's a key principle to bear in mind when writing description: **where possible, make your description work for you multiple times over.** By that I mean, can your description highlight something more than just imagery? A part of personality, perhaps something symbolic, maybe a character's belief, their quirk, or a moral quandary.

No matter your preference, there are some occasions where using description heightens the experience for a reader. For example:

- Using description when you need to clarify something complex.
- When you want to show rather than tell.

- When you need to add detail.
- When something is unusual.
- An emotional scene.
- Worldbuilding.
- When you want to focus your readers' attention on a particular scene, action or moment.
- When your protagonist is interested in something.

The Hero Lens

"Everything the hero does, sees, feels and thinks, encloses your reader into a tiny literary lens. Nothing happens in your book unless your protagonist experiences it. Everything is channeled through her. She is the lens your reader looks through when reading your story." Sacha Black, *10 Steps to Hero: How to Craft a Kickass Protagonist.*

Your hero's lens is made up of four parts:

- Actions
- Thoughts
- Dialogue
- Feelings

Now, getting the hero lens right isn't just about ensuring you write action or dialogue or thoughts for your hero. It's about *how* you write them. You need to understand how and why your hero sees things differently to every other character. What makes your character's viewpoint unique?

Your first exercise is to choose a descriptively heavy book and read it; and then choose a descriptively light book and read it. Note the books below:

Descriptively heavy:

-

-

-

Descriptively light:

-

-

-

Now use the space below to reflect on both books, what did you like or dislike about the prose? Where do you feel you would like your prose to sit compared to their levels of description?

-

-

-

-

-

Think about your current protagonist, what makes their viewpoint unique? Note down some things about their personality and history that makes the way they see the world unique.

-

-

-

-

-

-

Write a scene where your protagonist views a fight. Take the elements
from the previous exercise and let them influence your word and
grammar choices.

-

-

-

-

-

-

-

-

Now take your villain, antagonist or a character with the polar opposite views to your protagonist. Rewrite the fight scene from their perspective. Let them watch the fight and have their viewpoint influence your word and grammar choices.

-

-

-

-

-

-

-

-

-

Review both scenes and note your thoughts below. Prompt questions:

- Do they sound alike or different?
- What techniques did you use to create the effects?
- What can you take from this to use in your prose moving forward?

Write an emotional scene where a police officer tells a parent their child has passed away. Include as little description as possible.

-

-

-

-

-

-

-

-

Read the scene back and note your thoughts. Do you feel emotionally invested in the scene?

-

-

-

-

Now rewrite the scene including description, body language, visceral reactions etc.

-

-

-

-

-

-

-

-

-

Review both versions, which one do you feel is more emotionally impactful and importantly, why?

-

-

-

-

Vagueness

Vagueness is a plague on your descriptive writing. A lack of detail doesn't mean vague. Vague means unclear. Like this:

Sometime later, we arrived in the glade and set up camp.

Write as many vague phrases and sentences as you can. I'll start you off with two:

Later on, we...
There was something on the table...

Write a scene using the phrases above, your prompt is: the field.

-
-
-
-
-
-
-
-

Now rewrite the scene removing every instance of vagueness and replacing it with something specific.

-
-
-
-

.

.

.

.

.

Specificity

Detail—and I mean specific detail—slows the pace of your story. A valid technique, if you want to create a distraction or red herring. In characterization terms, when something is important to the hero they'd naturally spend longer on that subject. Let's put this into practice.

"We're done," she said, putting her glass on the table and walking out.

Might seem innocuous enough, but likewise, it doesn't evoke much of anything. There's no emotion or tension in the sentence. So what about this instead:

"We're done," she said, slammed her glass on the table and marched out.

Here, we've swapped out "put" and "walked" for slammed and marched. Two verbs that evoke much more than their predecessors.

When you add specific details to action—personal details with clear motivations behind them—it makes the action all the more powerful, bringing the argument to life. Like this:

"We're done," she said.

I hoped she'd put her glass on the table. But she cocked her head at it, narrowing her eyes. I lusted after those crystal tumblers for months before I could afford them. Instead of whiskey in plastic cups, it made the lads' poker nights something special. She hated poker as much as she hated the lads. I reached for the glass, but as my fingers neared the rim, she looked me straight in the eye and dropped it.

"Oops," she said, as it shattered on the floor. She didn't even look down. She just marched out, the glass crunching under her heels.

Write an unspecific sentence about looking in the mirror.

-

-

-

-

Now add just one detail to that sentence.

-

-

-

-

Now add a slew of details and reflections to the original sentence.

-

-

-

-

-

-

-

Reflect on all three, which one feels the most engaging and why? What techniques did you use to create the effects you've made?

-

-

-

-

Introducing Characters

Readers want to get to know characters through gradual discovery, not slapstick captain obvious lines. When you bring a new character into a scene for the first time, readers need just enough information to picture them without an information dump. Start with one or two unusual physical details your protagonist notices that no one else would. For example, some of the things I noted for, Dorian, one of my characters are the following:

Physical: brown mop-like curly hair, watery green eyes with a black ring around the iris, wears green suits.

Unusual: When he uses his power, he has a silver shimmer to his skin, he walks with a cane, both of which become important to the plot.

For your two main characters and your villain, note down three physical aspects and three unusual ones:

Protagonist

Physical:

1.

2.

3.

Unusual:

1.

2.

3.

Character 2

Physical:

I.

2.

3.

Unusual:

I.

2.

3.

Villain

Physical:

I.

2.

3.

Unusual:

I.

2.

3.

Put those elements into a description. Write a short scene where a new character meets each of your above characters. How do those aspects get woven into the description?

Protagonist

-

-

-

-

-

-

-

Character 2

-

-

-

-

.

.

.

.

Villain

.

.

.

.

.

.

.

Review the scenes above. Did you include a consequence of the physical aspects? For example, rather than just observing someone's white teeth, perhaps they make your character afraid because they're pointy as well as white. Or perhaps the smile makes their insides flutter.

Rewrite the above descriptions and include a consequence or impact of one of the aspects you're describing.

Protagonist

-

-

-

-

-

-

-

-

Character 2

-

-

-

-

-

-

-

-

Villain

-

-

-

-

-

-

-

Personality Traits

Personality traits are huge giant beasts that need wrangling into the depths of a character. So how do you wrestle these massive concepts down into something vivid and descriptive enough so that readers "see" your character's personality without actually slapping them around the chops with a telling statement?

Action darling, action.

Rather than writing a scene and stating a character is jealous, *show* their jealousy through their actions. For example, doing something underhand to the character they're jealous of. Saying something bitchy, etc.

Write a scene using action to demonstrate a character's jealousy. You're not allowed to use the word jealousy in the scene.

.

.

.

.

.

.

.

.

.

.

Write a scene using action to demonstrate a character's anger. You're not allowed to use the word anger in the scene.

.

.

.

.

.

.

.

.

.

.

.

Write a scene using action to demonstrate a character's negative mindset. You're not allowed to use the word negative in the scene.

.

.

.

.

.

.

.

.

.

.

.

STEP 8 SENSORY SCHMENSORY, EMOTION POTION

The books that have had the biggest impact on me aren't the ones that made me invest in the characters, though of course, I loved those books. The books that had the biggest impact are the ones that made me *feel*, the ones that made me cry and reflect on life and have emotional epiphanies. But how do you create emotions at the sentence level?

Well, one of the most important factors are including the senses.

Take the simple example below:

No Senses:

As the night draws in, he puts his arms around me and kisses me.

With Senses:

I lose myself in his arms. The forest, the chirping of nocturnal insects, and the rustling of the undergrowth all disappear as his lips touch mine.

Write your own kiss below, you're not allowed to use the senses to describe it.

-

-

-

-

-

-

-

-

-

-

Now rewrite the kiss using the senses:

-

-

-

-

-

-

-

-

-

-

-

Which kiss felt more real to you and why?

-

-

-

-

-

Smell Sense

As with metaphors and similes, the point of using the senses is to evoke the familiar. There's no point describing some obscure smell that only a chemist or perfumist would recognize. This is about relating the obscure to the familiar to bring a sense of clarity to the reader.

Describe the scent of death.

-

-

-

-

-

-

-

-

-

-

-

Describe the scent of love.

-

-

-

.

.

.

.

.

.

.

.

Describe the scent of fear.

.

.

.

.

.

.

.

.

.

.

.

With a lot of the senses, describing them is one thing, but it's the consequence to the character that's the most interesting bit for the reader.

Name a smell that means something to your protagonist (do they like it or loathe it?).

.

.

.

.

.

How does that smell or smells make your character feel?

.

.

.

.

.

What memories does your character recall linked to that smell or smells?

-

-

-

-

-

How is this smell important to the plot?

-

-

-

-

-

Write a scene where your protagonist encounters the smell.

-

-

-

-

-

-

-

-

-

-

Edit the scene and layer the smell with a descriptive technique like a simile and a consequence.

-

-

-

-

-

-

-

.

.

Sound Sense

Sound is often underused in fiction too. I've always wondered why that's the case when sound is used so prolifically in movies. Whenever there's rising tension in a film, the music grows louder (or higher pitched) until it crescendos. Or what about when there's no sound at all? That's just as bad. Sound is a tricky little schmuck because it's so often precluded by filtering (see Step 3 Where We Cock Up in Style).

Broadly, filtering is where you remove the reader one step from the protagonist. Instead of letting the reader see through the eyes of the protagonist, you show the reader the action the protagonist is doing. For example:

Filtering:

She heard the crunch of leaves.

Not Filtering:

Leaves crunched behind her.

Write a sentence with filtering. Your prompt is: engine.

.

.

.

-

-

-

-

-

-

-

Rewrite the sentence without filtering.

-

-

-

-

-

-

-

-

-

Onomatopoeia is referenced in the devices section as a key tool for creating both sound and image pictures. Which is why I'm mentioning it here. Adding crashes, wallops, and booms create sound in your prose.

Write a list of as many onomatopoeic words as you can think of below.

-
-
-
-
-
-
-
-
-

There are also other more subtle ways to evoke lyrical sound. Alliteration is another example. As too are other forms of alliteration, like repeating vowel or consonant sounds in a sentence like this:

Her heart ached and languished in the agonizing reality that he was gone.

Write a sentence about childbirth using alliteration.

-

-

-

-

Write a sentence using alliterative repetition of sounds to create a sound effect. Your prompt is: toddler.

-

-

-

-

Write a paragraph about a group walking through the woods, try to include as much sound as possible.

-

-

-

.

.

.

.

Write a short scene where you use silence to change the atmosphere. Your prompt is: window.

.

.

.

.

.

.

.

.

Taste Sense

Food isn't the only occasion where you can use taste as a sense in your writing. Like sound, there are loads of occasions you can use taste that you might not think of at first glance. For example, tasting emotions is a powerful way to create imagery and evoke emotion in the reader. Have you ever been so angry your mouth dries and tastes poisonous? Or perhaps you bite your tongue and taste the metallic heat of blood. Or maybe in a banging shag fest your lover's skin tastes sweet like honeyed milk. Smell, like taste, and the other senses, while predominantly their own, are connected to all the others. So where one sense is activated you might find activating another helpful to enrich your imagery.

List as many different tastes as you can think of in the space below, I'll start you off:

Bitter

Sweet

.

.

.

.

.

.

.

.

.

.

.

.

.

.

.

Write a sentence describing the taste of wind, only use the taste sense.

.

.

.

Write a sentence describing the taste of love, only use the taste sense.

.

.

.

Write a sentence describing the taste of hate, only use the taste sense.

.

•

•

Write a sentence describing the taste of pain, only use the taste sense.

•

•

•

Rewrite the above sentences, this time including at least one other sense.

•

•

•

Write a sentence describing the taste of wind.

•

•

•

Write a sentence describing the taste of love.

•

•

·

Write a sentence describing the taste of hate.

·

·

·

Write a sentence describing the taste of pain.

·

·

·

Touch Sense

Touch is a personal act, when you allow yourself to be touched—*stop it, don't be dirty*—even if it's as innocuous as a handshake, you make yourself vulnerable. You allow someone into your personal space. This is why moments of touch in a novel can be so evocative and not just for romance. Equally, the cool touch of a blade's edge can be just as effective at drawing a reader in, as a fingertip grazing a shoulder blade.

Touch, while mostly reflected in the connection our fingertips have with objects, can also be with our mouth's. Eating involves a plethora of textures like crunchy or squelchy or gritty or a range of others. Food is universal, every human on the planet has to eat to survive. So like emotion, when elements are universal, they require less written effort to bring the imagery alive.

Touch isn't just about texture, such as coarse or rough. Within touch there are other aspects like heat, pain, pleasure, and vibrations.

Write a sentence describing something that's not typically warm, and incorporate heat.

.

.

.

Write a sentence describing an object that unexpectedly vibrates.

.

.

.

Write a sentence about the first time a lover touches their love interest.

.

.

.

Write a short paragraph describing the taste, texture and sensations of your favorite meal.

.

.

.

Here are some unexpected ways you can include touch in your stories:

Buildings: buildings have an array of opportunities to describe textures from glass and brickwork and the structural foundations of the building to the furnishings and objects inside.

Weather and air: the sun can burn or warm, the wind can caress or ravage, the rain can patter on the arms or pound the body with hail and the air can be dry or humid.

Ground: the ground can squelch with treacherous mudslides, it can undulate or be rough and hard.

Skin: can be rough, brittle, leathery, or smooth.

Weapons: sharp blades, cool barrels, or the smoothed, polished wood of a mace handle.

Clothes: fabrics are a great way of including textures as there are so many from smooth silks to rough hessians, soft fleeces, and rubbery wetsuits.

Nature: nature is the ultimate texture haven, plants have thorns, rose petals are silky, some plants are furry.

Emotions: you might not think of emotions as having a texture, but they do! Think about the hot, throbbing of rage, or the cold, prickle of fear.

Take each one of the above examples and describe it ensuring you use touch:

Describe an unusual building.

-

-

-

-

-

Describe the weather.

-

-

-

-

-

Describe the ground.

-

-

-

-

Describe a character's skin.

.

.

.

.

.

Describe a weapon.

.

.

.

.

.

Describe clothes.

.

.

.

.

.

Describe nature.

-

-

-

-

-

Describe the following emotions: Jealousy.

-

-

-

-

-

Emotional hurt (love).

-

-

-

-

Excitement.

.

.

.

.

.

Emotions and Prose

Humans are complex animals. We don't just feel one thing, we habitually feel multiple emotions. For example, when a loved one has been in pain for a long time, we often feel relief as well as sadness when they pass. A dichotomy of conflicting emotions, but ones that convey emotions more deeply than single feelings.

"The more explosive 'outer' emotion should be shown through action and dialogue. The inner emotion should be shown through thought and body language." Sacha Black, *10 Steps to Hero: How to Craft a Kickass Protagonist.*

Write a scene where a character feels conflicting emotions.

.

.

.

.

.

-

-

-

-

-

Write a scene where your character feels something they shouldn't. Flip the expected emotion on its head.

-

-

-

-

-

-

-

-

-

Self-judgment is a great way to increase the emotion in a scene. Especially when your protagonist is making judgements about themselves against their moral compasses. *The best person to torture a protagonist isn't the villain, but themselves. We are usually our own worst critics and so self-judgment and self-criticism are an excellent way to torture a protagonist especially if they've broken one of their morals or values.*

Write a scene where your protagonist judges themselves for what they've done.

.

.

.

.

.

.

.

.

.

.

We're going to layer up the scene. Rewrite the scene digitally this time, you'll need lots of space as it will expand. Include the following elements:

- If they did do something wrong, what do they think they could/should have done differently?
- Include a memory or experience that helps them reflect on the situation.
- How can they justify—one way or another—what they've done?
- Can you create a metaphor or analogy describing the emotion or layered emotions?
- Include a detail, nuance or reflection that your hero notices in this moment that no one else would.

Review both scenes. Which one do you feel is more emotive? Which elements gave the scene the most depth? What lessons will you take from this into your prose going forward?

-
-
-
-
-
-
-
-

Fear in Prose

Aside from the hero's desire, fear is one of the key drivers in many novels. It drives the plot, pace, tension, and emotion. Which, when you combine those elements, creates the climax of your story. How do you create fear in your prose? Fear, like all emotions, is sensory.

With each emotion, the sensory reactions are different. For example, when you're afraid, the blood drains from your face turning it white, you blink rapidly, and beads of sweat run down your back tightening your muscles. Your villain—whether it's intangible conflict, an inner demon, a monster, or otherwise—should provoke that sort of reaction in your protagonist.

There are two main types of fear you can evoke in a story: psychological and physiological fear.

Psychological fear is about the **emotional state your characters (and therefore your readers) are in.**

But physiological fear is more about **violence, gore, torture, or anything gruesome.**

Tricks to showing fear include:

- Describing visceral reactions
- Describing body language changes
- Pathetic fallacy
- Missing items
- Sudden changes
- Fight/flight/freeze
- Withholding information

At the prose level, to create some of these affects you can use:

- Ellipsis (...)
- Cut dialogue off with em dashes (—)
- Interruptions
- Sudden changes in atmosphere

Write a scene using psychological fear.

-

-

-

-

-

-

-

-

-

Now rewrite the same scene using physiological fear.

-

-

-

-

-

-

.

.

.

.

Write a scene showing fear. Concentrate on using visceral body reactions and body language to show your character's fear.

.

.

.

.

.

.

.

.

.

.

Edit the scene and focus on using pathetic fallacy to add atmosphere.

.

-

-

-

-

-

-

-

-

Edit the scene and focus on leaving out crucial pieces of information, or the unknown to enhance your character's fear.

-

-

-

-

-

-

-

·

·

·

Edit the scene one final time. Include one of the original unused tricks for creating fear and also focus on prose level tricks.

·

·

·

·

·

·

·

·

·

Review all the scenes, which technique do you think created the biggest impact and why? What will you take from these scenes into your writing going forward?

·

.

.

.

Love in Prose

Love, like fear and like any other emotion, can be done in as many ways as there are author voices. The important thing is to embrace your style, whether that's lyrical and poetic or clean and sharp.

The other thing to note is, no one is saying you need to have full blown orgies in your book. A hand hold can be just as romantic as a fade to black or an R-rated erotic scene.

Love is the most sensual of all emotions so capitalizing on the senses in your prose is vital. As is using small details to reflect big emotions.

Love is huge, but when you break it down, just like fear, there are two key aspects you can describe to get big bangs for your bucks: the psychological aspect of love and the physiological aspect.

The psychological aspect of love is all about how the brain feels, the all-consuming mental emotions, the connection, the security; it's also about the character processing their understanding of what love means.

Think about how you can reflect the slow build both physically and psychologically at the sentence level. The longer the description, the longer the reader has to wait until they get to that kiss moment. Drawing out the prose and lengthening the psychological reflection and description in these moments becomes a tease to your reader itself. You can also subtly increase this effect by using longer sentences with more punctuation, using more specific verbs and increasing the number of metaphors and devices.

Write a character's first kiss.

·

·

·

·

·

·

·

·

·

·

Edit the kiss, focus on using the senses to describe the sensations of the kiss.

·

·

·

·

·

·

-

-

-

-

Write a scene where there's no sexual action but you're still conveying desire.

-

-

-

-

-

-

-

-

-

Edit the last scene where there's no sexual action, sprinkle small details only the protagonist would notice and use them to convey big emotions.

.

.

.

.

.

.

.

.

.

Now write a scene where your protagonist gets to undress their love interest, focus on sensual feelings and sensations. Note, they do not get to have sex! Focus on body language and visceral body reactions to demonstrate the emotion in the scene.

.

.

.

.

.

.

.

.

.

.

Write a scene where your protagonist confesses their love for another character. Focus on the dialogue beats between the lines of speech and make sure you use the tricks you've discovered like visceral body reactions and the senses.

.

.

.

.

.

.

.

.

.

STEP 9 PHILOSOPHY, POETRY, AND QUOTABLE PROSE

Not everyone wants or needs to write quotable prose and that's okay. If you write pulp fiction, for example, readers don't care about remembering specific, beautiful sentences. They're coming to your books for hard and fast story, wicked characters, and pure escapism. And that's totally fine. **Expressionism** as a movement spans art as well as poetry. It's concerned with the meaning of emotional experiences. **Expressionism in poetry specifically looks at raw emotions in everyday life.** This is one of the reasons I think it's so useful for writers to study. Story is about the emotional change the protagonist goes through. Emotion is what hooks a reader and expressionist poetry distills those emotional experiences into single sentences. But what does expressionist poetry look like? Here's one I made earlier:

"Love is the fire that burns when everything else is ash." Sacha Black, *Rebel Poetry*.

Try and write an expressionist poem about death.

.

•

•

Try and write an expressionist poem about love.

•

•

•

Defamiliarization is the art of presenting something old in a new unfamiliar way with the purpose of enhancing perception and understanding. Imagine great-grandmother Ethel rocking life in leathers and leopard print. The unusualness of representation but with the familiarity and comfort of nanny underneath is what creates the refreshing prose.

Here's another one I wrote using defamiliarization:

> "She liked the way her scars looked. They reminded her she'd won."
> Sacha Black, *Rebel Poetry*.

Try and write an expressionist poem about death using the defamiliarization technique.

•

•

•

Try and write an expressionist poem about love using the defamiliarization technique.

-

-

-

Use a juxtaposition to create an expressionist poem.

-

-

-

Deep Philosophy

Part of creating quotable prose is about going deep. You have to strike a chord with thousands of people simultaneously, which seems impossible. But the amazing thing about going deep and specific on an emotion or topic is that it becomes universal. Emotions connect humanity. If you want to deepen your prose by using specificity to create universality, consider covering abstract and philosophical themes or emotions like:

- Love
- Hope
- Fear
- Jealousy

- Death
- Loss
- Religion
- Faith
- War
- Sacrifice
- Freedom
- Power
- Justice

If one of these topics particularly relates to your story theme, even better. Whatever your book theme is, create philosophical questions around it. If you can't think of any questions, have a Google, there are lots of lists of philosophical questions online. Create two questions for each of the concepts above. Here are some examples to start you off:

- Is it really love if it's unrequited?
- What does death mean for life?
- If freedom is being able to do what you want, are wild animals freer than humans?
- Does power corrupt?

Love

Q1

Q2

Hope

Q1

Q2

Fear

Q1

Q2

Jealousy

Q1

Q2

Death

Q1

Q2

Loss

Q1

Q2

Religion

Q1

Q2

Faith

Q1

Q2

War

Q1

Q2

Sacrifice

Q1

Q2

Freedom

Q1

Q2

Power

Q1

Q2

Justice

Q1

Q2

Symbolism

There's a trick here for writers. The scenes you'll find the best opportunities for creating beautiful quotable prose are the most emotional and significant ones. If you like working with symbolism, there are always opportunities to find symbolism or significance.

Choose a moment in your book and examine the detail. How does that detail impact your hero's emotions and life?

Write down five seemingly insignificant details you could use in your book to symbolize a greater meaning.

1.

2.

3.

4.

5.

In your hero's vulnerable moments, what is significant to them?

.

.

.

.

.

.

.

-

-

-

What detail will your character remember more than anything else, even if it seems insignificant?

-

-

-

-

-

-

What visceral reactions does their body have?

-

-

-

-

-

.

What can they smell, taste, hear in this moment?

.

.

.

.

.

.

How does this moment change your hero's understanding of themselves?

.

.

.

.

.

.

How does that subsequently affect their motives and drivers?

-

-

-

-

-

-

What realizations or deeper understandings about the world does this give your protagonist?

-

-

-

-

-

-

What does your protagonist wish she could do or change or say but can't?

-

-

-

-

-

-

STEP 10 CRACKING THE CHARACTER CODE

There are many aspects to good characterization, but three I hold more important than all others:

- Emotion
- Choice
- Uniqueness

Constantin Stanislavski was a Russian actor, and director. He developed a model to train actors on how to improve their characterization in order to make their portrayal of the written characters more believable. So we're going to reverse engineer this technique to improve our characters and, specifically, the prose we wrap around them. Stanislavski's system was built on the principle of actors embodying characters to the extent the actor became not the character, but himself, as though the character were real. There are three key aspects to his method: "experience," "what if," and "motivation." We're going to explore all three.

Experience

The most significant driver behind Stanislavski's system was an actor's emotional memory. For actors, their ability to draw on their past experiences was paramount for Stanislavski. It is for us word monkeys too. When you're writing a scene, do you pull on past memories and experiences to create a sense of realism and depth in your characters?

Write down three emotional moments in your life.

Moment 1

.

.

.

.

.

Moment 2

.

.

.

.

.

Moment 3

-

-

-

-

-

-

Now expand on those moments. Write some thoughts around how you felt, what was significant, and how your body felt.

Moment 1

-

-

-

-

-

Moment 2

-

-

.

.

.

.

Moment 3

.

.

.

.

.

.

What if?

Writers use the "what if" question all the time to create plot ideas: what if the sky was really a hologram? What if my protagonist got hit by a car? What if her husband murdered her lover? But Stanislavski believed actors should ask themselves *what if* they were in the same situation as the character they were portraying.

Let's start playing the what if game.

Your character is 12 years old and stood at a T-junction in the middle of a road. Create three what if situations.

What if...

.

.

.

.

What if...

.

.

.

.

What if...

.

.

.

.

The same character now aged 18, has a choice between doing the right thing for the wrong reason, or doing the wrong thing for the right reason... Create three what if scenarios.

What if...

.

.

.

.

What if...

.

.

.

.

What if...

.

.

.

.

Look at your protagonist at the climax of your story. Write down four alternative ways the situation could go:

What if...

.

.

·

·

What if...

·

·

·

·

What if...

·

·

·

·

What if...

·

·

·

·

Motivation

Motivation is at the core of every character. Readers see through characters without a motivation faster than they can close your book. Motivation is a character's "why." It's the reason they exist. The reason they push the plot on to achieve their goal. Without it there's no meaning to their actions. Stanislavski was right. It's not just actors that need to know the motivation of their characters. We writers do too. Does your hero want to take down the villain for revenge? Is it because he's fallen in love? Or perhaps he wants to protect his people. Whatever the motive, there must be one for every action and reaction he makes in your story.

A character wants to kill their husband. Write down three different motivations for why they want to commit murder.

Motivation 1

-
-
-
-

Motivation 2

-
-
-
-

Motivation 3

-

-

-

-

A character wants to steal an object from their uncle. Why?

Motivation 1

-

-

-

-

Motivation 2

-

-

-

-

Motivation 3

-

.

.

.

Now look at your protagonist. What is the motivation behind their goal or the climax?

Motivation:

.

.

.

.

Goal:

.

.

.

.

Story Climax:

.

.

-

-

Use "what if" to come up with two alternative motivations.

What if...

-

-

-

-

What if...

-

-

-

-

Creating Uniqueness

One effective way of creating uniqueness in characters is through the use of quirks. But quirks are often confused with habits and there's a distinct difference between the two:

Habits

"A habit is a routine movement, action or behavior often done in a repeated pattern. It's automatic and something a reader would deem normal. For example, pushing your glasses up, checking the doors are locked before bed or always reading the newspaper in the morning." Sacha Black, *10 Steps to Hero: How to Craft a Kickass Protagonist.*

Quirks

"A quirk is unique and idiosyncratic to your character; it's a deliberate behavior. Usually, it will stick out to your reader or other characters. For example, in the movie *East is East*, one character, a young boy called Sajid, refuses to take his jacket off, EVER. He wears it rain, snow, sun or sleeping." Sacha Black, *10 Steps to Hero: How to Craft a Kickass Protagonist.*

Robert McKee in *Story,* discusses the concept of a character diamond. This is where you can identify a character based on hearing three aspects of their personality.

For example:

1. Addict
2. Genius
3. Socially awkward

There's only one character that describes: Sherlock Holmes. When grouped together, these personality aspects filter down to create an array of Sherlock's quirks. For example, his addict aspect creates the quirk of him smoking a pipe. His socially awkward trait means he enacts quirky behaviors others find odd, like sniffing and licking things and generally being unable to hold down effective relationships—unless they're work colleagues. And perhaps a combination of all three aspects mean he's wildly messy in life but his mind is a logical deductive mean machine.

There are two important aspects to creating believable quirks:

- The first is to ensure it has a function in your story.
- The second is to show rather than tell the quirk.

Write down 3 to 5 *habits* your protagonist has.

1.

2.

3.

4.

5.

Write down 3 to 5 *quirks* your protagonist has.

1.

2.

3.

4.

5.

What function will each of these quirks play in your story?

1.

2.

3.

4.

5.

Do the same for your villain.

Write down 3 to 5 habits your villain has.

1.

2.

3.

4.

5.

Write down 3 to 5 *quirks* your villain has.

1.

2.

3.

4.

5.

What function will each of these quirks play in your story?

1.

2.

3.

4.

5.

Now do the same for your two main side characters.

Write down 3 to 5 *habits* side character 1 has.

1.

2.

3.

4.

5.

Write down 3 to 5 *quirks* side character 1 has.

1.

2.

3.

4.

5.

What function will each of these quirks play in your story?

1.

2.

3.

4.

5.

Write down 3 to 5 *habits* side character 2 has.

1.

2.

3.

4.

5.

Write down 3 to 5 *quirks* side character 2 has.

1.

2.

3.

4.

5.

What function will each of these quirks play in your story?

1.

2.

3.

4.

5.

Create character diamonds for these four characters.

Protagonist

1.

2.

3.

Villain

1.

2.

3.

Side Character 1

1.

2.

3.

Side Character 2

1.

2.

3.

Introducing Characters

I need to make an itty, bitty point about introducing characters. I can't tell you the number of stories I read where characters aren't described the first or even second time we meet them but much later in the story. But by that point, the reader has already established a picture of the character.

I see a lot of manuscripts where writers only employ one method of description: describing what their protagonist "sees." For example, a new character with blonde hair wearing a floor-length coat comes into the scene and that's exactly what the writer describes. I mean... it works, and hey, perhaps the coat has some interesting features. But that doesn't tell you who this new character is.

What's more interesting to the reader is how this character makes the protagonist feel. When you come to describe a new character, ask yourself a key question:

When the character leaves the scene, what one thing do you want the reader to remember about them?

For 10 of your characters, note down how they will make your protagonist feel and what you want your readers (and or your protagonist) to remember about them, and then write a short description as if it were the first time they entered the story.

Character 1

Feelings

.

.

.

Memory

-

-

-

Description

-

-

-

-

-

-

Character 2

Feelings

-

-

-

Memory

-

-

-

Description

-

-

-

-

-

-

Character 3

Feelings

-

-

-

Memory

-

-

-

Description

-

-

-

-

-

-

Character 4

Feelings

-

-

-

Memory

-

-

-

Description

-

-

-

-

-

-

Character 5

Feelings

-

-

-

Memory

-

-

-

Description

-

-

-

-

-

Character 6

Feelings

-

-

-

Memory

-

-

-

Description

-

-

-

-

-

-

Character 7

Feelings

-

-

-

Memory

-

-

-

Description

-

-

-

-

-

-

Character 8

Feelings

-

-

-

Memory

-

-

-

Description

-

-

-

-

-

-

Character 9

Feelings

-

-

-

Memory

-

-

-

Description

-

-
-
-
-
-

Character 10

Feelings

-
-
-

Memory

-
-
-

Description

-
-

.

.

.

.

Reminder Touches

Once you've introduced a character, it's important to keep reminding the reader about their appearance while ensuring you mix up the description. For example, let's take the character Bob. Bob has blue eyes that your protagonist notices the first time he comes on the page. One day the sun shines, making his blue eyes even brighter. If Bob's mood changes, his eyes darken to a deep ocean blue.

For the most important five characters, think of three other ways you can describe them later in the story.

Character 1

1.

2.

3.

Character 2

1.

2.

3.

Character 3

1.

2.

3.

Character 4

1.

2.

3.

Character 5

1.

2.

3.

Deeper Description

Let's go deeper with describing the impact a character has on the protagonist. Below are the same three descriptions demonstrating specificity as in Step 6. This time we're going to look at them in a different context.

Description 1:

He was average height with brown eyes and a hard stare.

Description 2:

He slipped through the crowd unnoticed, his height allowing him to slide behind taller bodies. I caught his intense brown eyes and faltered. They were so dark they were almost black.

Description 3:

He was of average height—average everything, to be honest. Except his eyes. They were such a dark brown they almost looked black. But what struck me was what they held, a knowing; he'd seen death. *No.* I glanced again. It was darker than that. His eyes called to death, clutching it like a play thing. I stiffened as he passed and vowed never to cross him.

Example 1 is a perfectly valid description. But it's dismally vague and boring and if we're brutally honest, it doesn't create much of a picture in your mind. Example 2 has put his—what could be boring —average height into action and shown the consequence of it. Instead of just being "average" height, he's cunning and uses his average height to slip through a crowd like a ghost. All of a sudden, a boring feature is interesting. Example 3 is so much more interesting than the first two. He still has the same dark eyes and average height, but now he's interesting because not only has the protagonist noticed him, she feels something about him. In this paragraph she has both a mental reaction: noticing that he harbors death in his eyes, but also a visceral bodily reaction, stiffening as the character gets close.

Take your above five characters and answer three more questions, then write a passage of description for each one.

Character 1

What are the consequences of the aspect you want to describe?

-

-

-

-

What detail does your protagonist notice about this character that no one else would?

-

-

-

-

What is unexpected about this character?

-

.

.

.

Character description from your protagonist's perspective.

.

.

.

.

.

.

.

Character 2

What are the consequences of the aspect you want to describe?

.

.

.

·

What detail does your protagonist notice about this character that no one else would?

·

·

·

·

What is unexpected about this character?

·

·

·

·

Character description from your protagonist's perspective.

·

·

·

·

·

·

·

Character 3

What are the consequences of the aspect you want to describe?

·

·

·

·

What detail does your protagonist notice about this character that no one else would?

·

·

·

·

What is unexpected about this character?

-

-

-

-

Character description from your protagonist's perspective.

-

-

-

-

-

-

-

Character 4

What are the consequences of the aspect you want to describe?

-

-

.

.

What detail does your protagonist notice about this character that no one else would?

.

.

.

.

What is unexpected about this character?

.

.

.

.

Character description from your protagonist's perspective.

.

.

-
-
-
-
-

Character 5

What are the consequences of the aspect you want to describe?

-
-
-
-

What detail does your protagonist notice about this character that no one else would?

-
-
-
-

What is unexpected about this character?

-

-

-

-

Character description from your protagonist's perspective.

-

-

-

-

-

-

-

STEP 11 SELF-EDITING

In a way, much of this book is about the art of self-editing. It's about hacking and pruning your words until they sing sweet, sweet prose.

The two main forms of editing are: **revising and editing**. Together, they are the sisters that create prose perfection. But they're different processes and they achieve different things.

Revising involves sorting out the big picture. It uses the big picture brain rather than the detailed brain. It involves making sure:

- Your story flows.
- The pace and structure right.
- Your characters have a solid character arc and sufficient depth.
- You've closed off all the story threads.
- The tension is solid throughout the story.

We all have different ways of working, and some writers will do both of these things simultaneously. As long as you're finishing books, that's all that matters. But typically, it's easier to revise first: fix the big problems then work down to the sentence level.

Editing, however, is nittier and grittier. Editing requires a more detailed brain and digs deep into your sentences enabling you to polish that prose to perfection. It involves:

- Checking grammar and punctuation.
- Removing typos.
- Checking for consistencies and continuity.
- Fact checking.
- Correcting formatting errors.

Below is a check list. You can download a reusable version by joining my mailing list here: sachablack.co.uk/prosedownload

Self-Editing Checklist

When conducting a self-edit, it's important to check a variety of aspects of your novel. The below is a checklist reminder of what to check when you review your manuscripts.

Have you varied the amount of white space you have on each page?

Yes

No

Are there pages of dense prose versus pages of rapid-fire dialogue?

Yes

No

Is there variation of sentence length?

Yes

No

Have you used longer sentences where you want to draw out and slow down the pace?

Yes

No

Have you shortened sentences in action scenes?

Yes

No

Are you varying the rhythm and flow of sentences?

Yes

No

Do you have dense detail where things are important?

Yes

No

Have you checked the level of worldbuilding detail. Is it sufficient and not overdone?

Yes

No

Is there any unnecessary information-dumps?

Yes

No

Have you used sufficient detail to draw a reader's attention to one particular area (if needed)?

Yes

No

Have you applied light or no detail where you want narrative summary to move the story onwards or where things are less important?

Yes

No

Are there enough breadcrumbs in your manuscript and early enough for your Reader's subconscious to pick up on the clues?

Yes

No

Have you used symbolism or other literary tricks to make the fore-shadowing subtle?

Yes

No

Did you trial and test all POVs and tenses before starting to write your manuscript?

Yes

No

Have you done a full read through for consistency checks?

Yes

No

Have you checked for character continuity errors (height, weight, eye color)?

Yes

No

Have you created a file for this kind of character information?

Yes

No

Are there variations in the type of prose opening and closing chapters?

Yes

No

Is every chapter opening anchored in time, space and POV?

Yes

No

Have you checked your character list and made sure you don't have too many character names starting (or ending) with the same letter or sounds?

Yes

No

Have you slowed down your prose when something is important to your protagonist or when it's an intensely emotional scene?

Yes

No

Do you describe emotional moments in detail?

Yes

No

Do you skim over the things that aren't important like transitions and elapses of time?

Yes

No

Have you described your characters within a few paragraphs of them being introduced to the story?

Yes

No

Are you dropping breadcrumb reminders about your character's physical appearance and their personality throughout the rest of the story?

Yes

No

Have you turned potentially boring features into interesting ones by describing the consequences of that feature?

Yes

No

Have you changed a character's name too often or given them too many nicknames?

Yes

No

Have you checked for (and removed where possible) any instances of naming an emotion?

Yes

No

Have you scanned your verbs to check their strength?

Yes

No

Where you have weak verbs, have you strengthened them?

Yes

No

Have you checked your sentences don't always start with I, he, she or a character name? You can switch these around quickly by starting with the action in that sentence.

Yes

No

Have you removed as many instances of filtering as possible?

Yes

No

Have you checked your sentences to see whether there are any words that can be removed without the sentence losing its meaning? If you can remove them without affecting the sentence, do.

Yes

No

Are your sentences overcomplicated?

Yes

No

Have you repeated descriptions or overused phrases?

Yes

No

Do you repeat plot points or personality traits?

Yes

No

Are character names, sounds or letters repeated?

Yes

No

Have you checked for crutch words?

Yes

No

Have you checked your manuscript for uses of ing and as? If you have lots on a page, try and remove some.

Yes

No

Have you deleted instances of passive voice?

Yes

No

Have you removed complex negatives?

Yes

No

Have you kept a balance of foreign, made-up or technical words to ensure they enhance rather than confuse the story?

Yes

No

Have you checked for any descriptions that don't make logical sense? Remember, there's nothing quiet or soft about a lion's roar; they wanna eat you, they don't want to pet you.

Yes

No

Have you reviewed your dialogue to ensure your characters aren't naming each other too frequently?

Yes

No

Have you checked for overuse of dialogue tags, especially adverb tags?

Yes

No

Have you read through your dialogue and made sure your characters aren't interrupted repeatedly?

Yes

No

Do your tags match the tone of your dialogue?

Yes

No

Do you have a balance of inner monologue in your prose?

Yes

No

Have you differentiated the dialogue between characters?

Yes

No

Have you removed unnecessary exposition in your dialogue?

Yes

No

For your dialogue tags, are you using predominantly said or says? If you're using lots of descriptive words or action tags try and reduce the number.

Yes

No

Have you checked your use of contractions and used them where possible?

Yes

No

STEP 12 LITERARY HOLY GRAILS

We writers are lucky. There are lots of tools, techniques, and devices at our fingertips, ready and waiting for us to pluck their little demonstrative selves out of our literary toolboxes and dot their inky bodies onto the page. Whether it's alliteration, metaphors, or an Oxford comma, there's hundreds of the little fellas desperate to be used.

The whole of The Anatomy of Prose textbook book examines a range of tools and techniques, some more in-depth than others. But here, we're going to whip through a round of practicing with some of the most frequently used tools at our fingertips. Think of it as a pick and mix of literary pot luck.

Point of View (POV)

Point of view (POV) is perhaps the most key device to consider before you start your novel. I say "before" because I learnt the hard way that deciding you don't like the POV you've written your novel in after the fact is a bitch to correct.

Use the sections below to write the opening of your novel in each POV.

First Person POV.

-

-

-

-

-

-

-

-

-

-

-

-

-

-

-

-

-

-

-

-

-

Second Person POV.

-

-

-

-

-

-

-

-

-

-

-

-

-

-

-

-

-

-

-

-

-

Third Person Limited POV.

-

-

-

-

-

-
-
-
-
-
-
-
-
-
-
-
-
-
-
-

Third Person Omniscient.

-

-

-

-

-

-

-

-

-

-

-

-

-

-

-

.

.

.

.

Review all four openings, which do you like best? Which POV flows best? Which sounds most like your character's voice?

.

.

.

.

.

.

Fourth Wall Breaks

Breaking the fourth wall means a character will acknowledge the fact they're a character and speak directly to the audience. **Fourth wall breaks are best used when readers least expect it.** *Deadpool*, for example, uses it in the opening scene in the middle of an action fight scene. Something that's supposed to be fast-paced and continuous until there's a winner.

Write a scene where your protagonist breaks the fourth wall and speaks directly to the reader.

-
-
-
-
-
-
-
-
-
-
-

Allusion

Allusion occurs when an author refers to another character or event or literary work within their story with the aim of adding depth and context—for example, if your character was shouting at another character and said something like:

"You're not Peter Pan, Jim. Grow up."

Be warned though, if your reader doesn't know who you're refer-ring to, you'll lose them and the purpose of the allusion is gone. Therefore, using extremely well known references is advisable.

Write five instances of allusion using your protagonist.

1.

2.

3.

4.

5.

Juxtapositions

One of my favorite quotes of all time is a juxtaposition. I think juxtapositions might be my personal literary obsession; they're so flexible and create a huge amount of depth in your writing. **A juxta-position is when you place two things close together or side by side, for the purpose of comparison or contrast.** You can use juxta-positions on a macro or micro level.

Macro Juxtapositions

If you think about it, the hero in just about every book written is a juxtaposition himself. He starts out flawed, but by the end of the book is whole again. Likewise, when you create your hero's goal, you normally juxtapose what they want with what they have to do to get it. Which creates the conflict that drives the plot.

Micro Juxtapositions

On the micro scale, you can use juxtapositions in description and worldbuilding, sentences, dialogue, narration, and inner thought. It's also a handy technique for evoking emotion and deepening characterization. In fact, I'm struggling to think of a single place you can't use a juxtaposition!

Here's an example that I use frequently to explain juxtapositions:

"Beneath the beauty and the charm and the sharp sparkle of her personality, she had a core of steel. She was like a blade wrapped in a bouquet of orchids. I hoped to god whoever took her made the mistake of underestimating her." Melissa Albert, *The Hazel Wood*.

In this example, there are contrasting comparisons a-plenty. Beauty and charm are pitted against the sharpness of the character's personality. There's a weapon (a blade) which is then contrasted against the softness of petals and flowers.

Juxtapositions are particularly effective at evoking emotion because humans are complex. We often feel multiple emotions at the same time.

Make some notes about your hero's macro juxtaposition.

.

.

.

.

.

.

.

.

.

Write a descriptive juxtaposition describing an emotion.

.

.

.

.

.

Write a descriptive juxtaposition describing a different emotion.

.

.

.

.

.

Write a descriptive juxtaposition describing three different characters.

Character 1

.

.

.

.

.

Character 2

.

.

.

.

.

Character 3

.

.

.

.

.

Foreshadowing

Foreshadowing involves doing your best Hansel and Gretel impression. Successful foreshadowing drops tiny breadcrumbs in key places throughout your story for readers to pick up. If done correctly, it's like really good foreplay. It preps and builds readers up for your climax. Which should... if you've primed them well enough, leave them wholly satisfied and... erm... breathless!

Loaded Guns

There's a physical form of foreshadowing that Anton Chekov referred to as a loaded gun.

"One must never place a loaded rifle on the stage if it isn't going to go off. It's wrong to make promises you don't mean to keep." Chekhov, letter to Aleksandr Semenovich Lazarev (pseudonym of A. S. Gruzinsky), 1 November 1889.

Every word you write, every sentence you type is a promise from you to your readers. Readers place their attention in your hands. If you show them something, they naturally assume it's of relevance. If you describe a door, readers will expect your protagonist to walk through it.

Write down five things you need to foreshadow in your story.

1.

2.

3.

4.

5.

How Do You Foreshadow?

Warnings, advice, black cats, metaphors, similes, any literary tool you use to describe one thing when you really mean another, can be used to symbolize or foreshadow something else.

The white dove that flies past at the end of a battle scene: foreshadowing. Beauty and the Beast's red rose? Foreshadowing. The red and roses represent love and the falling petals foreshadow the potential doom of the beast.

Taking those five things you noted in the last exercise. Expand on them and write down 3 ways you could foreshadow each thing.

Thing 1

1.

2.

3.

Thing 2

1.

2.

3.

Thing 3

1.

2.

3.

Thing 4

1.

2.

3.

Thing 5

1.

2.

3.

Priming the reader before they know what your story is about sets them up to accept your ending subconsciously. The art of foreshadowing is telling your reader's subconscious what's coming, whilst keeping their conscious mind in the dark. One key way of doing this is to show rather than tell.

Write a short description showing the foreshadowing of each of the 5 things you've chosen in the previous exercises.

Thing 1

Thing 2

Thing 3

Thing 4

Thing 5

Misdirection

Misdirection is like oxygen for foreshadowing. It's essential. That said, you can't misdirect everyone. Some readers know a genre so intimately it's almost impossible to pull the wool over their eyes. But you do need to *try* and misdirect your readers enough they're put off the scent of your true reveal. Word of caution, though, my little Sherlocks —this is about balance, misdirect a reader too much and they disbelieve your ending.

Note down 3 ways you could misdirect the reader for each item you want to foreshadow.

Thing 1

1.

2.

3.

Thing 2

1.

2.

3.

Thing 3

1.

2.

3.

Thing 4

1.

2.

3.

Thing 5

1.

2.

3.

The Big Reveal

It might sound obvious, but... if you're going to lay down bread-crumbs you actually need to use them. If you don't, a reader's subconscious can be an irritating little swine and make their conscious mind feel like strings have been left untied.

For each element you want to foreshadow, note down how you will reveal it in your story.

Thing 1

Thing 2

Thing 3

Thing 4

Thing 5

Sentence Length

Playing with sentence length makes me giddy, it's another of my favorite techniques. Varying the sentence length allows you to reflect the protagonist's mood. For example, if you wanted to reflect a frantic, chaotic emotion aka my usual state, you could shorten the sentences, have single word sentences, cut speech off or over-use commas. For example:

> My breath is hollow. It roars. Thunderous vibrations fill my ears. The gun is heavy; my finger though, is steady. My heart thuds. Once. Twice. Three times. Then I pull the trigger.

Use sentence length to create a sense of anger in your character.

.

.

.

.

.

Use sentence length to create a sense of desire in your character.

.

.

.

.

.

Use sentence length to create a sense of thoughtfulness in your character.

.

.

.

.

.

Metaphors and Similes

Metaphors and similes are similar. They do the same job and for the most part, we all live in blissful ignorance of the difference between them. But, there is a difference.

- A simile describes something as *like* something else.
- A metaphor says something *is* something else.

But which one is best? Well, both are excellent devices to use in your prose, but if you're asking which one packs a bigger literary atom bomb, then read the following two sentences and decide for yourself:

- **Simile:** My child is like a monster.
- **Metaphor:** My child is a monster.

Create a metaphor and simile describing a person's face.

Metaphor

Simile

Create a metaphor and simile describing hatred.

Metaphor

Simile

Create a metaphor and simile describing love.

Metaphor

Simile

Alliteration

Dictionary.com describes alliteration as the following:

"The commencement of two or more stressed syllables of a word group either with the same consonant sound or sound group."

Alliteration, while commonly found in successive words, doesn't have to be consecutive like "Colin's Car." It can be found in famous book titles like *Gone Girl, The Two Towers, Black Beauty, Pride and Prejudice, The Great Gatsby, Fahrenheit 451, East of Eden, The War of the Worlds,* the list goes on.

You can also create alliteration by using several words in a sentence using the same letters or sounds but spaced a little apart. Here are two examples from Bram Stoker's *Dracula*.

"The castle is a veritable prison, and I am a prisoner!" Bram Stoker, *Dracula*.

"...What devil or what witch was ever so great as Attila, whose blood is in these veins?" Bram Stoker, *Dracula*.

Think of four instance of alliteration you could use in your current novel.

1.

2.

3.

4.

Create a sentence describing someone you know using an instance of alliteration.

.

.

.

Edit the description and overuse alliteration.

.

.

.

Review both. Edit and tweak the overused version until you get to a satisfactory level of alliteration where it feels flowing and not ridiculous.

Plosive Letter Choice

Plosive letters, also sometimes called stop consonants, are ex*plosive* letters that block the air in your lungs ceasing air flow. They quite literally explode from the mouth like a firework on acid. It creates an interesting effect in prose.

Plosive letters include: b, d, g, t, k, and p.

A quick succession of plosives can create a sharp effect. The most obvious example of this is swear words. For example: bitch, shit, bastard, fuck, twat, and dick to name but a few of my favorite oral delectables. While not everyone likes their usage, swear words tend to be used in highly emotive situations like when you hurt yourself or when you're pissed; conveniently, those are great times to spit fireworky rage.

Write a scene where your character is angry, try to use a range of plosive letters and words to impact the effect.

.

.

.

.

.

.

Onomatopoeia

Dictionary.com defines onomatopoeia as:

"The formation of a word, as *cuckoo, meow, honk,* or *boom,* by imitation of a sound made by or associated with its referent."

In other words, a word that sounds like it's meaning. Like crash or boom or bang.

Write down as many onomatopoeic words as you can in the space below.

.

.

.

.

.

.

.

-
-
-
-
-

Take five of the words above and dissect them. Do they create a long sound and effect like boom which mushrooms out for as long as you keep the mmm sound going? Or are they short like bang, which comes to a sudden stop just like the action?

Word 1

Word 2

Word 3

Word 4

Word 5

Write an action scene, a fight perhaps, and use as many onomatopoeic words as you can.

.

.

.

.

.

.

.

.

.

.

.

.

Anthropomorphism and Personification

Anthropomorphism occurs when you give human qualities to something that's not human. For example, the weather, animals, or objects. Here, though, the meaning is literal. Examples include Winnie the Pooh and all his friends, Simba from the Lion King, and the Animals from Animal Farm. With all of these examples, the non-human thing behaves in a human way, be it by talking or by being jealous or otherwise.

Personification, while still giving non-human things human-like traits, it's less literal and more figurative. "Money talks," "lightning danced," "alarm clocks yelling," and "work calling" are all examples of personification.

Think of two famous examples of anthropomorphism.

1.

2.

Write a short scene where you use anthropomorphism, your prompt is: zoo.

.

.

.

.

.

.

.

.

.

Think of five things or objects you can personify and write a sentence personifying them.

Thing 1 Personification Sentence.

Thing 2 Personification Sentence.

Thing 3 Personification Sentence.

Thing 4 Personification Sentence.

Thing 5 Personification Sentence.

Pathetic Fallacy

Pathetic fallacy is multifaceted. It's a device in and of itself but it can be used as a form of foreshadowing. What is pathetic fallacy? Well, playing with the weather—you know, when it gets all dark and cold and thundery, and you're all *pillow on face* summat baaads about to happen.

Think of five types of weather and what they could symbolize or fore-shadow and then write a sentence foreshadowing just that.

Weather 1

Foreshadowing

Foreshadowing Sentence

Weather 2

Foreshadowing

Foreshadowing Sentence

Weather 3

Foreshadowing

Foreshadowing Sentence

Weather 4

Foreshadowing

Foreshadowing Sentence

Weather 5

Foreshadowing

Foreshadowing Sentence

Oxymoron

Oxymorons occur when you place two conflicting words next to each other to describe the same thing. For example, bittersweet, old news, lead balloon, living dead, perfect mistake.

Think of five oxymorons and note them below.

1.

2.

3.

4.

5.

Anaphora

Anaphora is the intentional use of repetition. Specifically used at the beginning of a series of clauses or sentences. There are lots of famous examples in poetry and speeches. One such example is from perhaps the most famous speech ever made:

> "**I have a dream** that one day this nation will rise up and live out the true meaning of its creed... and **I have a dream** that one day on the red hills..." Martin Luther King, 1963.

This particular example is famous for its emotional resonance and the empowerment it inspired in so many people.

Create a paragraph using anaphora, your prompt is: town mayor.

-
-
-
-
-
-
-
-

.

.

.

Isocolon

You create an isocolon when you repeat a phrase, sentence, or clause of equal length that also has similar rhythms to it. For example:

> "It was the best of times, it was the worst of times, it was the age of wisdom, it was the age of foolishness," Charles Dickens, *A Tale of Two Cities.*

Create a paragraph using Isocolons, your prompt is: loss.

.

.

.

.

.

.

Hyperbole

I like hyperbole, it's fun and dramatic and a little diva-ish. Hyperbole is exaggeration. It's not meant to be taken literally. You might notice a certain author uses hyperbole a lot... ahem. Whenever I think of hyperbole, I mostly picture a teenager flinging her arms around while telling her friends about the latest drama.

> "Oh my god, Luce. You won't believe it, he kissed me like eight million times."

Write a short scene with a diva for a character using hyperbole as a tactic.

- .

- .

- .

- .

- .

- .

Malapropism

Malapropism is a nifty little comedic tool. Malapropism is the replacing of a word with similar sounding (but wholly incorrect) words. For example, "don't upset the apple cart" would become "don't upset the apple tart."

Another example would be: "I'm not to be trifled with" which could become "I'm not to be truffled with."

Malapropisms are lighthearted and funny because they create a faux pas in speech and usually at the most inopportune times. This tool is great for lighter stories with humorous characters. Not so good, however, for dropping into prose that's more serious.

Write a humorous scene where a character uses malapropisms.

.

.

.

.

.

.

.

WANT MORE?

There's just three more things to say before you go:

First of all, you can get your exclusive reusable self-editing checklist by signing up to my mailing list by visiting: bit.ly/sachaML

Don't forget to download your FREE resource guide, the reading list, and a bunch more useful things. You can get that by visiting: sachablack.co.uk/prosedownload

Secondly, I hope you found this book helpful in your quest to craft better sentences. If you liked the book and can spare a few minutes, I would be really grateful for a short review on the site from which you purchased the book. Reviews are invaluable to an author as it helps us gain visibility and provides the social proof we need to continue selling books.

Third, if you're looking for a supportive writing community, I run a Facebook group where I host a weekly accountability thread, writing prompts, and more. Join us here: facebook.com/groups/rebelauthors

From me to you, thank you for reading *The Anatomy of Prose Workbook* and good luck with your writing journey.

FURTHER READING

Read more of Sacha Black:

The Anatomy of Prose: 12 Steps to Sensational Sentences
13 Steps to Evil: How to Craft a Superbad Villain
13 Steps to Evil: How to Craft a Superbad Villain Workbook
10 Steps to Hero: How to Craft a Kickass Protagonist
10 Steps to Hero: How to Craft a Kickass Protagonist Workbook

Read more on grammar:

The Elements of Style by William Strunk Jr. and E.B. White
Eats, Shoots and Leaves by Lynne Truss

For more on literary devices:

The Elements of Eloquence by Mark Forsyth
Also a useful website is: literarydevices.net.

For more on writing craft:

DIY MFA: Write with Focus, Read with Purpose, Build your Community by Gabriela Pereira

Activate by Damon Suede a thesaurus of actions and tactics for dynamic fiction

Verbalize by Damon Suede

The Emotion Thesaurus series by Angela Ackerman and Becca Puglisi

Self-Editing for Fiction Writers, Second Edition by Rennie Browne and Dave King

Spellbinding Sentences: A Writer's Guide to Achieving Excellence and Captivating Readers by Barbara Baig

For expressionist poets to aid with quotable prose, I recommend reading:

Milk and Honey by Rupi Kaur

Love Her Wild by Atticus

Wild Embers by Nikita Gill

The Princess Saves Herself in This One by Amanda Lovelace

For flash fiction and micro flash fiction:

Hinting at Shadows by Sarah Brentyn

The Congress of Rough Writers: Flash Fiction Anthology Vol. 1 by Charli Mills et al. (you'll find a very early piece of flash in there from me too!

For creating fear:

Twisted, a story collection by Daniel Willcocks

The Ritual by Adam Nevill

For onomatopoeia

Lots of kids book recommendations!

We're Going on a Bear Hunt by Michael Rosen

Most Dr. Seuss books

For more on POV

Writing the Intimate Character by Jordan Rosenfeld

For Second Person POV specifically

The Language of Dying by Sarah Pinborough
Note here that I also recommend this book for a look at creating detailed emotions and beautiful prose.
The Fifth Season by N.K. Jemisin

ALSO BY SACHA BLACK

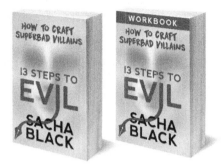

13 Steps To Evil - How To Craft A Superbad Villain (and Workbook) For Writers

Your hero is not the most important character in your book. Your villain is.

If you're fed up of drowning in two-dimensional villains and frustrated with creating clichés, this book is for you.

In **13 Steps to Evil,** you'll discover:

- How to develop a villain's mindset
- A step-by-step guide to creating your villain from the ground up
- Why getting to the core of a villain's personality is essential to make them credible
- What pitfalls and clichés to avoid as well as the tropes your story needs

Finally, there is a comprehensive writing guide to help you create superbad villains. Whether you're just starting out or are a seasoned writer, this book will help power up your bad guy and give them that extra edge.

If you like dark humour, learning through examples and want to create the best villains you can, then you'll love Sacha Black's guide to crafting superbad villains. Read 13 Steps to Evil and the companion workbook today and start creating kick-ass villains.

13 Steps To Evil How To Craft A Superbad Villain

13 Steps To Evil How To Craft A Superbad Villain Workbook

ALSO BY SACHA BLACK

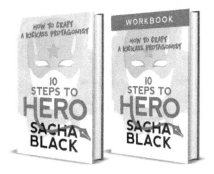

10 Steps to Hero - How to Craft a Kickass Protagonist (and Workbook) For Writers

From cardboard cut-out to superhero in 10 steps.

Are you fed up of one-dimensional heroes? Frustrated with creating clones? Does your protagonist fail to capture your reader's heart?

In 10 Steps To Hero, you'll discover:

+ How to develop a killer character arc

+ A step-by-step guide to creating your hero from initial concept to final page

+ Why the web of story connectivity is essential to crafting a hero that will hook readers

+ The four major pitfalls to avoid as well as the tropes your story needs

Finally, there is a comprehensive writing guide to help you create your perfect protagonist. Whether you're writing your first story or you're a professional writer, this book will help supercharge your hero and give them that extra edge.

These lessons will help you master your charming knights, navigate your way to the perfect balance of flaws and traits, as well as strengthen your hero to give your story the conflict and punch it needs.

First, there were villains, now there are heroes. If you like dark humor, learning through examples, and want to create the best hero you can, then you'll love Sacha Black's guide to crafting heroes.

Read 10 Steps To Hero today and start creating kick-ass heroes.

10 Steps To Hero: How To Craft A Kickass Protagonist

10 Steps To Hero - How To Craft A Kickass Protagonist Workbook

ABOUT THE AUTHOR

Sacha Black is an author, rebel podcaster, speaker and developmental editor. She has five obsessions; words, expensive shoes, conspiracy theories, self-improvement, and breaking the rules. She also has the mind of a perpetual sixteen-year-old, only with slightly less drama and slightly more bills.

Sacha writes books about people with magical powers and other books about the art of writing. She lives in Hertfordshire, England, with her wife and genius, giant of a son.

When she's not writing, she can be found laughing inappropriately loud, blogging, sniffing musty old books, fangirling film and TV soundtracks, or thinking up new ways to break the rules.

http://eepurl.com/bRLqwT

www.sachablack.co.uk
sachablack@sachablack.co.uk

instagram.com/sachablackauthor

bookbub.com/authors/sacha-black

facebook.com/sachablackauthor

twitter.com/sacha_black

amazon.com/author/sachablack

Made in United States
North Haven, CT
30 January 2023

31856322R00147